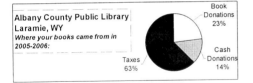

New Hampshire

THE THIRTEEN COLONIES

New Hampshire

CRAIG A. DOHERTY

KATHERINE M. DOHERTY

Facts On File, Inc.

New Hampshire

Facts On File, Inc.
132 West 31st Street
New York NY 10001

Library of Congress Cataloging-in-Publication Data
Doherty, Craig A.
    New Hampshire / Craig A. Doherty and Katherine M. Doherty.
        p. cm. — (Thirteen Colonies)
    Includes bibliographical references and index.
    ISBN 0-8160-5411-8 (acid-free paper)
    1. New Hampshire—History—Colonial period, ca. 1600–1775—Juvenile literature. 2. New Hampshire—History—1775–1865—Juvenile literature. I. Doherty, Katherine M. II. Title.

    F34.3.D64 2004
    974.2'02—dc22   2004005471

Facts On File books are available at special discounts when purchased in bulk quantities for businesses, associations, institutions, or sales promotions. Please call our Special Sales Department in New York at (212) 967-8800 or (800) 322-8755.

You can find Facts On File on the World Wide Web at http://www.factsonfile.com.

Text design by Erika K. Arroyo
Cover design by Semadar Megged
Maps and graph by Dale Williams

Printed in the United States of America

VB FOF 10 9 8 7 6 5 4 3 2 1

This book is printed on acid-free paper.

This book is dedicated to
the many students of all ages
we have worked with and taught over the years.

Contents

Note on Photos

Many of the illustrations and photographs used in this book are old, historical images. The quality of the prints is not always up to current standards, as in some cases the originals are from old or poor-quality negatives or are damaged. The content of the illustrations, however, made their inclusion important despite problems in reproduction.

Introduction

In the 11th century, Vikings from Scandinavia sailed to North America. They explored the Atlantic coast and set up a few small settlements. In Newfoundland and Nova Scotia, Canada, archaeologists have found traces of these settlements. No one knows for sure why they did not establish permanent colonies. It may have been that it was too far away from their homeland. At about the same time, many Scandinavians were involved with raiding and establishing settlements along the coasts of what are now Great Britain and France. This may have offered greater rewards than traveling all the way to North America.

When the western part of the Roman Empire fell in 476, Europe lapsed into a period of almost 1,000 years of wars, plagues, and hardship. This period of European history is often referred to as the Dark Ages or the Middle Ages. Communication between the different parts of Europe was almost nonexistent. If other Europeans knew about the Vikings' explorations westward, they left no record of it. Between the time of Viking exploration and Christopher Columbus's 1492 journey, Europe underwent many changes.

By the 15th century, Europe had experienced many advances. Trade within the area and with the Far East had created prosperity for the governments and many wealthy people. The Catholic Church had become a rich and powerful institution. Although wars would be fought and governments would come and go, the countries of Western Europe had become fairly strong. During this

Vikings explored the Atlantic coast of North America in ships similar to this one. *(National Archives of Canada)*

time, Europe rediscovered many of the arts and sciences that had existed before the fall of Rome. They also learned much from their trade with the Near and Far East. Historians refer to this time as the Renaissance, which means "rebirth."

At this time, some members of the Catholic Church did not like the direction the church was going. People such as Martin Luther and John Calvin spoke out against the church. They soon gained a number of followers who decided that they would protest and form their own churches. The members of these new churches were called Protestants. The movement to establish these new churches is called the Protestant Reformation. It would have a big impact on America as many Protestant groups would leave Europe so they could worship the way they wanted to.

In addition to religious dissent, problems arose with the overland trade routes to the Far East. The Ottoman Turks took control of the lands in the Middle East and disrupted trade. It was at this time that European explorers began trying to find a water route to the Far East. The explorers first sailed around Africa. Then an Italian named Christopher Columbus convinced the king and queen of Spain that it would be shorter to sail west to Asia rather than go around Africa. Most sailors and educated people at the time knew the world was round. However, Columbus made two errors in his calculations. First, he did not realize just how big the Earth is, and second, he did not know that the continents of North and South America blocked a westward route to Asia.

When Columbus made landfall in 1492, he believed that he was in the Indies, as the Far East was called at the time. For a period of time after Columbus, the Spanish controlled the seas and the exploration of what was called the New World. England tried to compete with the Spanish on the high seas, but their ships were no match for the floating fortresses of the Spanish Armada. These heavy ships, known as galleons, ruled the Atlantic.

In 1588, that all changed. A fleet of English ships fought a series of battles in which their smaller but faster and more maneuverable ships finally defeated the Spanish Armada. This opened up the New World to anyone willing to cross the ocean. Portugal, Holland, France, and England all funded voyages of exploration to the New World. In North America, the French explored the far north. The Spanish had

Depicted in this painting, Christopher Columbus completed three additional voyages to the Americas after his initial trip in search of a westward route to Asia in 1492. *(Library of Congress, Prints and Photographs Division [LC-USZ62-103980])*

already established colonies in what are now Florida, most of the Caribbean, and much of Central and South America. The Dutch bought Manhattan and would establish what would become New York, as well as various islands in the Caribbean and lands in South America. The English claimed most of the east coast of North America and set about creating colonies in a variety of ways.

Companies were formed in England and given royal charters to set up colonies. Some of the companies sent out military and trade expeditions to find gold and other riches. They employed men such as John Smith, Bartholomew Gosnold, and others to explore the lands they had been granted. Other companies found groups of Protestants who wanted to leave England and worked out deals that let them establish colonies. No matter what circumstances a

After Columbus's exploration of the Americas, the Spanish controlled the seas, largely because of their galleons, or large, heavy ships, that looked much like this model. *(Library of Congress, Prints and Photographs Division, [LC-USZ62-103297])*

colony was established under, the first settlers suffered hardships as they tried to build communities in what to them was a wilderness. They also had to deal with the people who were already there.

Native Americans lived in every corner of the Americas. There were vast and complex civilizations in Central and South America. The city that is now known as Cahokia was located along the Mississippi River in what is today Illinois and may have had as many as 50,000 residents. The people of Cahokia built huge earthen mounds that can still be seen today. There has been a lot of speculation as to the total population of Native Americans in 1492. Some have put the number as high as 40 million people.

Most of the early explorers encountered Native Americans. They often wrote descriptions of them for the people of Europe. They also kidnapped a few of these people, took them back to Europe, and put them on display. Despite the number of Native Americans, the Europeans still claimed the land as their own. The rulers of Europe and the Catholic Church at the time felt they had a right to take any lands they wanted from people who did not share their level of technology and who were not Christians.

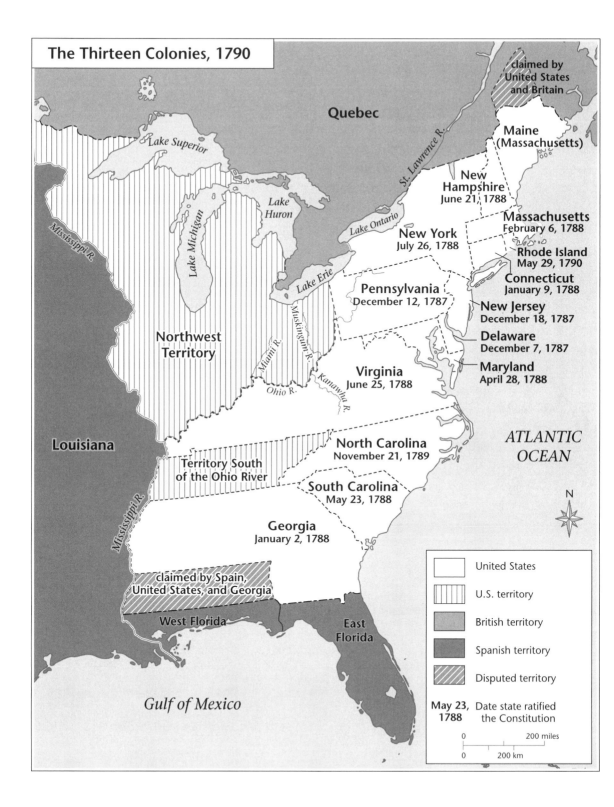

The Thirteen Colonies, 1790

Quebec

Lake Superior

Lake Michigan

Lake Huron

Lake Ontario

Lake Erie

Mississippi R.

St. Lawrence R.

claimed by
United States
and Britain

Maine
(Massachusetts)

New
Hampshire
June 21, 1788

Massachusetts
February 6, 1788

New York
July 26, 1788

Rhode Island
May 29, 1790

Connecticut
January 9, 1788

Pennsylvania
December 12, 1787

New Jersey
December 18, 1787

Delaware
December 7, 1787

Maryland
April 28, 1788

Northwest
Territory

Miami R.

Muskingum R.

Ohio R.

Kanawha R.

Virginia
June 25, 1788

Louisiana

North Carolina
November 21, 1789

ATLANTIC
OCEAN

Territory South
of the Ohio River

South Carolina
May 23, 1788

Georgia
January 2, 1788

N

Mississippi R.

claimed by Spain,
United States, and Georgia

West Florida

East
Florida

Gulf of Mexico

	United States
	U.S. territory
	British territory
	Spanish territory
	Disputed territory
May 23, 1788	Date state ratified the Constitution

0   200 miles

0   200 km

First Contacts

EARLY EXPLORERS

In the 16th and early 17th centuries, a number of European explorers sailed past New Hampshire's 15 miles of coastline, and fishermen from Europe fished in the waters of the North American coast. Some of these fishermen set up fishing camps, where they dried fish on the islands off the coast of Maine, on Cape Cod, and most likely on the Isles of Shoals off the coast of New Hampshire. The fishermen did not leave any records of their temporary settlements, and the explorers sailed south with little comment on what they passed. The first explorer to record his visit to what would become New Hampshire was Bartholomew Gosnold in 1602. Gosnold mapped the coast of New England from Maine south to Narragansett Bay in Rhode Island. Gosnold's map was used by many of the explorers and colonists who followed him.

Sassafras

The sassafras is a deciduous tree that grows as a bush and, as a tree, reaches a height of 50 feet. The bark on the root of a sassafras tree is used in medicine as both a stimulant and a diuretic. Oil of sassafras is extracted from the above-ground bark and is used in perfume and as a flavoring in a number of beverages.

In the early 1600s, Samuel de Champlain helped establish French claims in the New World. *(National Archives of Canada)*

In 1603, Martin Pring sailed to New Hampshire with two ships, the *Speedwell* and the *Discoverer*. His expedition was financed by a group of English investors who were interested in finding a source of sassafras trees, which were harvested for medicinal purposes. Pring sailed into the Piscataqua River. He did not find any sassafras trees there. He then sailed south to the site where the Plymouth Colony would later be established and found the sassafras he wanted. When he returned to England, Pring wrote a description of his voyage that was published and widely circulated.

Two years later, in 1605, the French explorer Samuel de Champlain sailed along the New Hampshire coast and landed on the Isles of Shoals. However, it was Captain John Smith who sailed along and mapped the coast that he named New England and who became the biggest promoter of the area. Smith returned from his 1614 voyage with a shipload of valuable furs and published his *A Description of New England*. The pamphlet was intended to entice people to settle in New England. He wrote in glowing terms about the land and climate of New England: "[T]he sea there near the Isle of Shoals is the strangest fish-pond I ever saw." He claimed the fishing in New Hampshire would be worth more than all the gold that explorers expected to find in Virginia. Despite Smith's glowing descriptions, New Hampshire was not an empty wilderness. A large population of Native Americans already lived in the area.

THE WESTERN ABENAKI OF NEW HAMPSHIRE

There are no accurate records of the number of Native Americans in the area that became New Hampshire. The best estimates suggest that as many as 5,000 Native Americans lived in the New Hampshire area. They are referred to as the Western Abenaki. They lived in six main groups. The locations of these groups have been assigned to them as tribal names. The Piscataqua were centered in what is now Dover. The Nashua lived in what is now Massachusetts

Captain John Smith mapped and named the New England coast and helped govern the Jamestown colony in Virginia. Author of many books about his exploration, Smith created this 1606 map of Virginia. *(Library of Congress)*

and New Hampshire, in the area around the present-day city of Nashua, New Hampshire. The Pennacook lived in the center of the state near modern-day Concord and Manchester. The Winnepesauke lived near the lake that bears their name. The Ossipee lived south of the White Mountains along the border between Maine and New Hampshire. The final group, the Coosuc, lived along the upper reaches of the Connecticut River, which forms the border between New Hampshire and Vermont.

The Western Abenaki spoke a dialect of the Algonquian language and belonged to a cultural group known as the Eastern Woodland Indians. The people of the Eastern Woodland culture

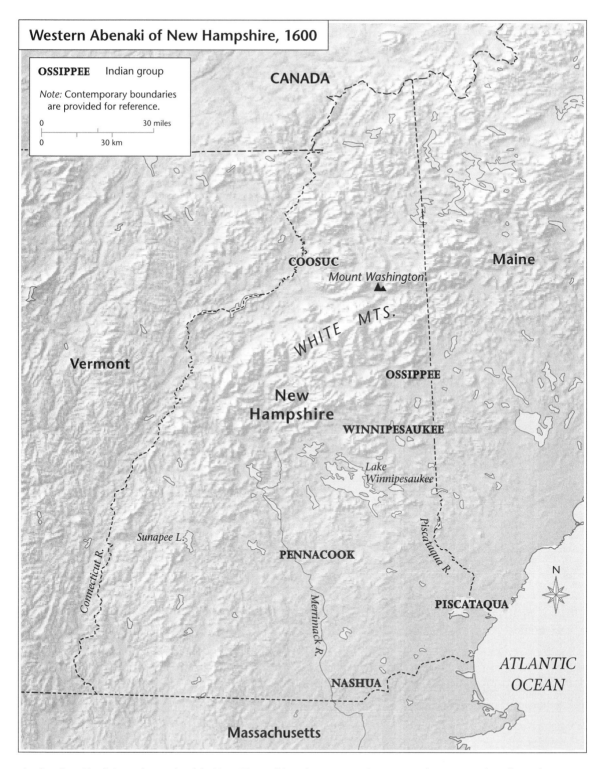

Western Abenaki of New Hampshire, 1600

OSSIPPEE   Indian group

Note: Contemporary boundaries are provided for reference.

0 ———————————— 30 miles
0 ———————————— 30 km

CANADA

COOSUC

Mount Washington ▲▲

WHITE MTS.

Maine

Vermont

OSSIPPEE

New Hampshire

WINNIPESAUKEE

Lake Winnipesaukee

Sunapee L.

Connecticut R.

PENNACOOK

Piscataqua R.

PISCATAQUA

Merrimack R.

N

ATLANTIC OCEAN

NASHUA

Massachusetts

At the time English settlers arrived in New Hampshire, there were six groups of Western Abenaki in the area.

This mid-19th-century illustration depicts Abenaki people bundled in many layers of clothing. The figure whose back is turned is carrying snowshoes. *(National Archives of Canada)*

depended upon the forest for much of their subsistence. They also were accomplished farmers who grew corn, beans, and squash. They supplemented their diet with game and fish that were abundant in the area.

THE SEASONAL LIFE OF THE WESTERN ABENAKI

The Western Abenaki had learned to take advantage of all that the forest around them had to offer. In the spring of the year, before the snow was completely gone, they would tap the maple trees and collect the first spring run of sap. The maple sap was boiled down to syrup that was used to sweeten their food. As the snow disappeared and the spring floods subsided in the rivers and streams, the annual spawning runs of a variety of fish took place. The Abenaki built weirs of stones in the rivers and streams that forced the fish to swim into their traps. The fish that were not eaten immediately were smoked for later. In addition to fishing from

Corn

Corn was first domesticated 6,000 to 8,000 years ago in Central America. Mesoamerican corn was *Zea mays* and Europeans called the crop maize or Indian corn. Its cultivation spread until it was being grown throughout the temperate regions of North America. Corn is a member of the grass family. Through careful seed selection and hybridization, Native Americans were able to develop many varieties of corn and adapt its growth to a wide range of climatic zones. In New England, the Native Americans grew three main varieties of corn. The most important type could be dried and ground into cornmeal to make a variety of dishes. They also grew a variety of corn that was dried whole and added to soups and stews throughout the winter. It was also eaten fresh, like modern corn on the cob. They also grew a variety of corn that was used as popcorn.

shore, the Western Abenaki also made canoes from birchbark. These boats were light and easily paddled. In addition to fishing, the canoes provided transportation on the region's many lakes, rivers, and streams. There was an extensive network of water routes throughout the area. Many of these were connected by trails known by the French word *portages*. The lightweight bark canoes could easily be carried across the *portages*.

The Western Abenaki would make special trips to find blueberries and other desired berries. *(U.S. Department of Agriculture)*

After the spring fish runs, it would be time to plant the fields. Like most Woodlands Indians, the Western Abenaki cleared their farmland by a technique known as slash and burn. When they needed to establish a new field, they would girdle the trees by cutting a strip of bark all the way around the base of the trees in the area they wanted to clear. This caused the trees to die. The area of dead trees would then be burned, creating an opening in the forest that would be used for farming. The fields of the Western Abenaki were planted with corn, beans, and squash in the same fields. The corn was planted with a few stalks grouped together in a small hill of soil. Beans were planted in the hills and their vines used the cornstalks for support. The squash were planted between the hills to efficiently use the space in the field.

In addition to the three main food crops, the Western Abenaki grew small patches of tobacco that was smoked in pipes during important ceremonies and meetings. During the summer, when they were not tending their fields, the Western Abenaki gathered a variety of berries. Blueberries were especially sought after, and groups would often make trips to areas where the berries were plentiful when they became ripe late in the summer. They also gathered raspberries, blackberries, and numerous other berries. As the season changed to fall, they would gather nuts and wild plants to store for the winter. Butternuts and chestnuts were their favorite nuts.

Once the fall harvest and gathering was completed, the people would begin to hunt. Deer, moose, bear, and many smaller animals were eaten by the native people of New Hampshire. Animals were not just

This illustration by Jonathan Carver shows the detail of a tobacco plant. The Western Abenaki grew this plant and smoked its leaves. *(National Library of Canada)*

important for food; every part of the animal served a purpose. Hides and furs were used for clothing, bedding, and footwear. The best moccasins were made from moose hide, and bear skins, with their thick fur, made warm winter robes or were used as blankets. The bones and antlers from the deer and moose were fashioned into a variety of tools.

Each group had an area they considered their hunting territory, and they would fight to keep rival groups from hunting in their area. They hunted using bows and arrows, stone knives, and spears. They would often hunt as a group and drive deer so that the deer

Some American Indians used deerskin as a disguise while hunting. This mid-16th-century engraving by Jacques Le Moyne depicts American Indians in what is now Florida employing this method. *(Library of Congress, Prints and Photographs Division [LC-USZ62-31871])*

would pass hidden hunters who could more easily shoot them with arrows. In the winter, the deer would gather into yards in stands of softwood trees where they were protected from the harsh New England winters. The Western Abenaki covered themselves with deer hides and wore antlers to sneak into the deer yards, where they could more easily kill the deer.

The Western Abenaki hunted moose in the fall. *(U.S. Fish and Wildlife Service)*

The northern groups of the Western Abenaki had more moose in their area than deer and would hunt them in the fall during the mating season. They would use moose calls made from birchbark to imitate the call of a bull moose. When a bull moose would hear the call, he would rush to it to defend his territory. In the winter, when the snow was deep, moose were hunted on snowshoes, a Native American invention. The hunters could stay up on the

Snowshoes

The snowshoes of the Western Abenaki would be recognizable to anyone who has seen or used modern wooden snowshoes.

They allowed the Indians to walk on deep snow without sinking in. Their snowshoes were made using a wooden frame that turned up in the front and was about three feet long and 16 inches wide. Webbing made of thin strips of deer hide was woven onto the frame. Straps were attached to the frame and then tied to the foot of the person using the snowshoes. Without snowshoes, the Native Americans of the Northeast would have found winter travel almost impossible.

This early 18th-century engraving shows Native Americans wearing snowshoes while hunting deer. *(Library of Congress, Prints and Photographs Division [LC-USZ62-115626])*

snow and were able to catch up with a fleeing moose and kill it with their spears.

WESTERN ABENAKI VILLAGES AND SOCIAL STRUCTURE

The Western Abenaki, like most Woodlands Indians, moved around their territory and had temporary and semi-permanent camps where they hunted, fished, and gathered wild foods. Their more permanent villages were usually located near their fields, and in the New Hampshire area were often close to one of the area's

In a late 19th-century engraving published in *Harper's Weekly,* some Native Americans relax near their birch-bark wigwams. *(Library of Congress, Prints and Photographs Division [LC-USZ62-106105])*

larger rivers or lakes. The waterways provided transportation as well as more fertile soil in the river valleys. The Western Abenaki villages varied in size from as small as 50 people to more than 500. Each village contained a number of family wigwams.

A wigwam is a small structure made by constructing a frame of flexible wooden poles made from green, or fresh, wood. The thicker ends of the poles were set in the ground in two rows 10 to 15 feet apart or were set in a circle. The poles were then bent into the middle and tied together to form either an arch or dome-shaped frame. The frame was covered with layers of bark to keep out the rain and snow. A hole was left in the center of the roof to let the smoke from the winter fires out. In the summer, the cooking fire was outside the wigwam. Often, several related families would build a longer version of the wigwam and live together.

Among the Western Abenaki, families were arranged in a patrilineal fashion. This means that when people married, they joined the husband's family, and the children became members of their father's clan. Clans are groups of people who share common ancestors, and each clan is represented by a different animal totem. Among the Western Abenaki, there were the bear, turtle, beaver, partridge, raccoon, muskrat, and hummingbird clans. It was against the social practices of the group for a young man or woman to marry anyone who was in their father or mother's clan.

Each group of Western Abenaki usually had two different chiefs. These chiefs were selected because of their personal abilities and often held their position throughout their lifetime. One chief was in charge of the day-to-day issues that faced the group. The other chief would be the leader in times of war, although until the coming of Europeans, there was little warfare among the Western Abenaki. If problems existed between the different groups, the chiefs would gather together in a council and work out a solution to the problem. In most Native American cultures, a problem would be discussed until everyone at the council came to an agreement on a solution. The chiefs did not vote in the way modern representatives do.

THE COMING OF THE EUROPEANS

The peaceful and healthy existence of the Western Abenaki and all the other Native Americans of New England was forever changed by the arrival of Europeans in the early 1600s. Before

Shamans were integral to the spiritual life and general health of many tribes. In this engraving, an Algonquian shaman prepares for a ritual or ceremony in a Plains Indian–style wigwam. *(Library of Congress)*

Native Americans and Disease

Most scholars agree that the ancestors of the Native Americans originated in Asia and traveled to North America when the two continents were connected by a land bridge between modern-day Siberia and Alaska. During the thousands of years they were isolated from the Asian and European continents, they lost or never developed any immunity to the diseases that the Europeans brought with them to North America.

Common diseases for Europeans like mumps and measles were often fatal for Native Americans. The most deadly disease, which had also killed large numbers of people in Europe, was smallpox. Smallpox epidemics ran through the Native American population of New Hampshire numerous times during the colonial period. Very few Native Americans survived smallpox.

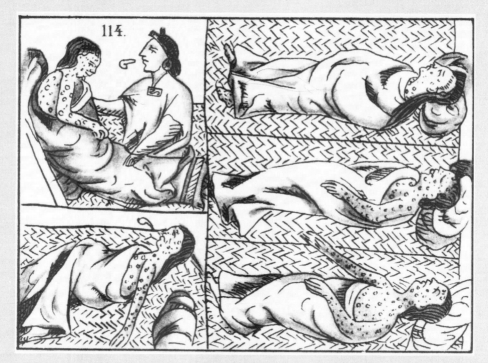

Published in *Historia general de las cosas de Nueva España* in the 1570s, this illustration shows Aztec people sick with smallpox. American Indians throughout the Americas suffered great losses from the influx of European diseases that accompanied colonization—especially smallpox. *(Library of Congress)*

any permanent settlers arrived, Native Americans began dying in large numbers from contact with European fishermen and explorers. In 1617, an epidemic of a European disease, which may have been smallpox, started in the area at the mouth of the Saco River (modern-day Biddeford, Maine). The disease spread rapidly up and down the New England coast and inland along the rivers.

It is estimated that only 5 to 10 percent of the Native Americans who were infected survived. It is because of this epidemic that the earliest European settlers were able to find choice sites along the coast where there were few or no Native Americans. If the Europeans had had to contend with the full pre-epidemic population of Native Americans, the small settlements of Plymouth Colony in Massachusetts and those in New Hampshire might not have been able to survive.

The effects of disease on the Western Abenaki were terrible, but that was not their only problem. They soon found themselves involved in a number of conflicts. As the colony's settlements grew, the Abenaki lost their lands. Competition over hunting lands with the Iroquois to the west led to many bloody fights in which the less powerful Abenaki often suffered the greater losses. As they were pushed northward by European settlers, the Western Abenaki found themselves forming alliances with the French traders and priests in Canada.

By the end of the 17th century, a series of wars broke out between the French and their Indian allies and the British colonists. Most of the Algonquian-speaking tribes of the Northeast, including the Western Abenaki, fought with and for the French. By the end of the French and Indian wars in 1763, almost all the Native Americans in New Hampshire had died of disease, been killed in war, or moved north into Canada.

2

First Settlements in New Hampshire

CREATING NEW HAMPSHIRE

At the beginning of the 17th century, England turned its attention toward the possibilities of profiting from its claim to most of the land in North America. The defeat of the Spanish Armada in 1588 had made the oceans safer for British ships, and the riches the Spanish had taken from New Spain had the English anxious to

Sir Ferdinando Gorges
(1566–1647)

Ferdinando Gorges was born in Long Ashton, Somersetshire, England, in 1566. When he was 26, he was captured by a ship in the Spanish Armada. After he was released by the Spanish, he joined the French forces that were fighting the Spanish. When he returned to England, he was knighted for his service in the war with Spain. In 1606, he became a member of the Plymouth Company that leased land to the Pilgrims in 1620 for the establishment of the Plymouth Colony in Massachusetts. Before that, in 1607, he had sponsored an attempt to establish a colony at the mouth of the Kennebec River in what is now Maine. That colony was unsuccessful in part because of the large population of Native Americans who were already in the area. In 1620, Gorges was instrumental in convincing the king to set up the Council of New England.

Captain John Mason
(1586–1635)

John Mason was born in King's Lynn, Norfolk, England, in 1586. Mason attended Oxford College and then joined the British navy in 1610. In 1615, he was appointed the governor of the colony at Conception Bay, Newfoundland. During the fishing season, thousands of fishermen from England and other countries fished in the waters off Newfoundland. Their success encouraged many to think about establishing other colonies in North America. Mason wrote about his experiences in Newfoundland in a pamphlet titled *A Briefe Discourse of the New-Found-land*. In it, he wrote that the "Cods [were] so thicke by the shore that we hardlie have been able to row the boate through them, I have killed them with a pike [spear]."

After five years as governor in Newfoundland, Captain Mason returned to England and became a member of the Council of New England, where he was able to use his personal experience to promote colonization in New England.

explore and develop the land they claimed. In England, numerous companies and government boards were set up to oversee the development of colonies in North America. One government-appointed agency was called the Council of New England, and it was in charge of making land grants and developing the lands that John Smith had named New England.

There were many notable and important Englishmen on the Council of New England. Two of the more active members were Sir Ferdinando Gorges and Captain John Mason. Mason had been the governor of a fishing colony in Newfoundland and knew the potential of the lands of New England. Gorges was very wealthy and thought he could profit by setting up colonies in North America.

In 1622, Gorges and Mason used their positions on the Council of New England to receive a grant of land in New England. Their grant was for the Province of Maine and gave them

> all that part of the main land in New-England lying upon the sea-coast betwixt ve rivers of Merrimack and Sagadahock [Kennebec] and to the furthest heads of the said rivers, and soe forwards up into the land westward until three-score miles be

finished from ye first entrance of the aforesaid rivers, and halfway over; that is to say, to the midst of the said two rivers web bounds and limitts the lands aforesaid together wit all the islands and isletts within five leagues distance of ye premises and abutting upon ye same or any part or parcell thereof.

Mason and Gorges also received two other grants. One was known as the Marianna Grant, and it gave them the land between

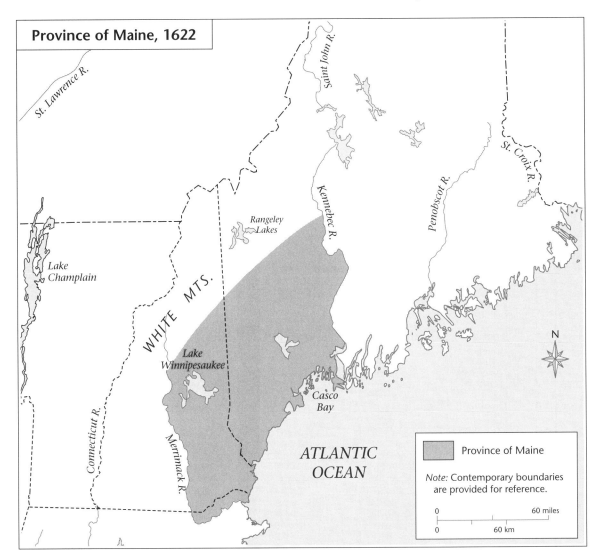

Province of Maine, 1622

The lands originally granted to Gorges and Mason were situated between the Merrimack and Kennebec Rivers and extended 60 miles inland.

the Merrimack River and the Salem River to the south. They also formed the Laconia Company, which received a grant of 1,000 acres along the shores of the Lake of the Iroquois. Some people assume this meant Lake Champlain; however, nothing was ever done with this grant and its actual location was never established.

THE FIRST EUROPEAN SETTLERS IN NEW HAMPSHIRE

The Plymouth Company had done little more than grant the Pilgrims the right to use land in North America. Those first settlers in New England suffered and many died during the first winter. When Mason decided to establish a colony in New Hampshire, he did not want to repeat the mistakes made at Plymouth Plantation. Rather than send out religious dissidents looking for a place to practice their religion, Mason's plan was to create a colony that was similar to an English estate.

In 1622, Mason and Gorges both hired people who were to go to New England and start developing their lands there. David Thomson led one group and landed at the mouth of the Piscataqua River in April 1623, where they set up the first settlement in New Hampshire. This was called Pannaway on what is now called Odiorne's Point. Today this area is part of Rye, New Hampshire. After a short time at Pannaway, this group moved to an area that was called Strawbery Banke because of the abundant wild strawberries there. This settlement continued and eventually became Portsmouth, New Hampshire. The second group was led by William and Edward Hilton, who were fish merchants from London.

The Hilton group went a few miles up the Piscataqua River and established a settlement, which was called Newichawannock. Later the name was changed to Dover, which it is called today. Unlike the Pilgrims, the first setters along the Piscataqua River were well supplied by their employers. Both groups set to work clearing land and making improvements that were expected to help the colony become profitable.

They built sawmills to turn the trees they cut into lumber. Some of the lumber was used to build houses, ships, boats, and other structures in the colony, while much of it was sent back to England. The largest trees in the colony, those over 24 inches in

Cod

Atlantic cod were extremely abundant in the waters off the northeast coast of North America. Cod were easily caught in the relatively shallow waters of the Grand Banks of Newfoundland and Labrador and Georges' Banks off the coast of New England. Basque fishermen, from what is now the Basque region of Spain, had perfected the technique of drying cod using salt, which made it possible for the fish to be transported great distances to be sold.

Along with the Basque came fishermen from England, France, and Portugal.

The fishermen would set up temporary camps along the coast, where they would dry the cod they caught. Once they had a boatload, they would sail back to Europe and sell their dried cod. The fish stages on the Isles of Shoals had been originally built by these European fishermen. As New Hampshire grew, fishing became an important part of the economy of the colony.

When the English discovered the abundance of Atlantic cod along the coast of the New World, many of them set up temporary settlements in which they could dry the fish to transport and then sell it. Detail of a 1715 map by Herman Moll, this illustration shows the process off the coast of Newfoundland. *(Library of Congress)*

diameter, were reserved for the Royal Navy and were sent back to England to be used as ships' masts. The colonists also built salt-works to evaporate seawater and get the salt. The salt was used to preserve cod and the other fish that they exported to England.

Fish stages, wall-less structures used to dry fish, were built on Great Island at the mouth of the Piscataqua River. The colonists also used the existing fish stages on the Isles of Shoals just off the coast. In addition, the settlers traded with the Western Abenaki for furs. Mason sent a herd of Danish cattle that had been specially selected for their ability to survive in cold climates like New England. Despite all this activity, the colony continued to be a losing proposition from a business standpoint. However, Captain Mason was committed to the success of his colony and eventually spent more than £22,000 on his efforts.

In 1629, Mason and Gorges decided to split the Province of Maine. Gorges's share was the land between the Piscataqua and Kennebec Rivers. Mason received sole title to all the lands from the Piscataqua south to the Merrimack. His family estates were near Plymouth, England, in the county of Hampshire. When he and Gorges split their grant, Mason called his share New Hampshire. It is estimated that there were 500 Europeans in New Hampshire by 1630.

In 1632, Captain William Neale, along with Darby Field and Henry Jocelyn, were sent out to see if they could find additional sources of revenue for Mason and the investors in the Laconia Company. They set out from Strawbery Banke and headed north toward the mountains in hopes of finding sources of metals or mineral wealth that the speculators in England had hoped for. They also hoped to contact more Native Americans and expand the colony's fur trade. Although they ran short of supplies and had to return to the colony without finding any gold or precious stones, they made it to the White Mountains and returned with tales about the wonders of the mountains and all they had seen there.

EXETER AND HAMPTON

Massachusetts grew much more rapidly than its neighbor New Hampshire. In 1630, both colonies had around 500 settlers. Just 10 years later, the population of New Hampshire had doubled to more than 1,000 people. Massachusetts was almost nine times

Anne Hutchinson's religious beliefs and practices were challenged in Massachusetts Bay Colony, from which she was banished. She fled to Providence Colony (present-day Rhode Island) with other people seeking religious freedom but later moved yet again to Long Island. *(Library of Congress, Prints and Photographs Division [LC-USZ62-53343])*

more populous, with more than 8,900 people, and there were more than 1,000 people in Plymouth Colony. There were also a number of people in Massachusetts who did not agree with how the religious leaders of the colony wanted people to worship. The Puritans had left England so they could worship as they wanted. This did not mean that they were willing to tolerate people who disagreed with them.

Rhode Island was established by Roger Williams and other dissidents from Massachusetts. The third town in New Hampshire was also established by people who disagreed with the religious leaders in Massachusetts. Anne Hutchinson had started a group in Boston that studied the Bible together and discussed their religious beliefs. Some of the ideas shared by this group upset the leaders in Boston, and they put Anne Hutchinson on trial. She was banished and joined the colony in Rhode Island. Her brother-in-law, John Wheelwright, was part of this group, and he also disagreed with the religious leaders in Boston.

Wheelwright thought that the Puritan leaders were too liberal and criticized them. He, too, was put on trial and banished. Rather than follow his sister-in-law to Rhode Island, Wheelwright and his parishioners moved north and set up a community on the Squamscott River, which empties into Great Bay, which they called Exeter. The settlers at Exeter drew up their own set of rules for the running of their community. This document is known as the Exeter Combination and was signed by Wheelwright and 34 others from the community.

There were a number of disagreements in England over exactly where the boundaries of different colonies were. Gorges and

The Exeter Combination
(1639)

Whereas it hath pleased the Lord to move the Heart of our dread Sovereigns Charles by the Grace of God King &c. to grant Licence and Libertye to sundry of his subjects to plant themselves in the Westerlle parts of America. We his loyal Subjects Brethern of the Church in Exeter situate and lying upon the River Pascataqua with other Inhabitants there, considering with ourselves the holy Will of God and o'er own Necessity that we should not live without wholesomne Lawes and Civil Government among us of which we are altogether destitute; do in the name of Christ and in the sight of God combine ourselves together to erect and set up among us such Government as shall be to our best discerning agreeable to the Will of God professing ourselves Subjects to our Sovereign Lord King Charles according to the Libertyes of our English Colony of Massachusetts, and binding of ourselves solemnly by the Grace and Help of Christ and in His Name and fear to submit ourselves to such Godly and Christian Lawes as are established in the realm of England to our best Knowledge, and to all other such Lawes which shall upon good grounds he made and enacted among us according to God that we may live quietly and peaceably together in all godliness and honesty.

Mason failed to establish claim to the Marianna Grant south of the Merrimack River, and the Massachusetts Bay Colony claimed that area. Gorges and Mason tried unsuccessfully to have the Massachusetts Bay Charter changed or revoked. At the same time, the leaders in Massachusetts claimed that their colony went north of the Merrimack into New Hampshire. The death of John Mason in 1635 made the situation in New Hampshire even more difficult.

To try and establish their claim, Massachusetts sent a group of settlers led by Stephen Bachiler, their Puritan minister, to build a fort and establish a town on the Winnicummet River. This settlement became Hampton, New Hampshire. The fact that New Hampshire was now made up of two Puritan towns full of people from Massachusetts and two towns established by Gorges and Mason led to a number of problems for the small colony. Many of the new residents in Dover and Portsmouth came to escape the strict life in Puritan Massachusetts. The leaders in Massachusetts took advantage of upheavals in Britain to take over New Hampshire in 1641. Although the four towns retained some of their separate

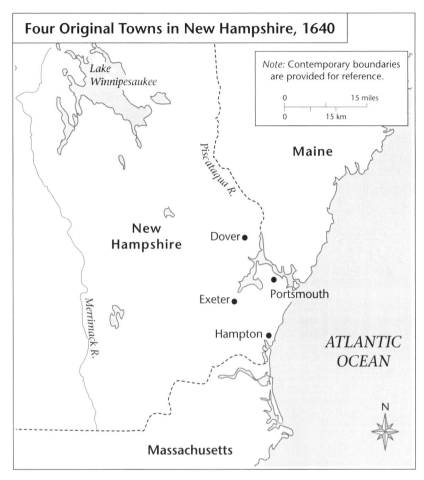

Four Original Towns in New Hampshire, 1640

Note: Contemporary boundaries are provided for reference.

0   15 miles

0   15 km

Lake Winnipesaukee

Piscataqua R.

Maine

New Hampshire

Dover●

●
Portsmouth

Exeter●

Merrimack R.

Hampton ●

ATLANTIC OCEAN

N

Massachusetts

Portsmouth (known at first as Strawbery Banke), Dover, Hampton, and Exeter were the four original English towns in New Hampshire.

rights, they would remain part of Massachusetts for 40 years. It would be 1673 before another town, Nashua, would be established in New Hampshire.

3

Conflicts with Native Americans

As New Hampshire became part of Massachusetts, they shared in the problems of their much larger neighbor. One of the most serious issues for all the people of New England was their relations with the remaining Native Americans of the area. All the land settled by Europeans had belonged to Native Americans. The land along the coast was all but emptied of Native Americans by the epidemic of 1617, but as the Europeans spread inland, conflicts with the remaining Native Americans became frequent. The Puritans in New England had no respect for people who did not share their religious beliefs, and they used the fact that the Native Americans had their own religions as an excuse to take the land they wanted. The Puritans' attitudes eventually led to a series of wars that eliminated even more of the Native Americans in New England. The first of these wars is known as the Pequot War.

THE PEQUOT WAR

As more and more people arrived in New England, they were encouraged to spread out up and down the coast. There were soon settlements north into what is now Maine and south into what would become Connecticut. In Connecticut, the settlers quickly spread out up the Connecticut River into territory that belonged to the Pequot tribe. The settlement of the Connecticut River Valley later led to the settlement of the western border of

New Hampshire. Saybrook, Connecticut, was established at the mouth of the river with a substantial fort. The communities of Wethersfield, Hartford, and Windsor in what would become Connecticut and Springfield in Massachusetts were all settled along the river, before the first major conflict with the Native Americans.

Both the leaders in Boston and those in the small Connecticut colony saw the advantage in taking over the fertile lands of the Connecticut River valley. They knew they would have to deal with the Pequot to do it. At first, they used the Pequot as trading partners. The colonists exchanged cloth and metal objects for furs. However, the Pequot had fought with many of their Native American neighbors before and after the coming of the English. They were not going to let more of their land be taken without a fight. As more and more settlers moved into Pequot territory, it was inevitable that there would be conflict.

The first strike in what would become known as the Pequot War is not clearly recorded. The leaders of the Massachusetts Colony considered the death of Captain John Stone in 1634, a trader of uncertain reputation, as the first strike in the war. Stone was killed by the Western Niantic who were allies of the Pequot. The leaders of the colony used the death of Stone as the reason to force the Pequot to sign a treaty with the colony that was unfavorable to them. Two years later, when another trader, John Oldham, was killed by Native Americans on or near Block Island off the coast of what became Rhode Island, Massachusetts sent an expedition of 90 men, led by John Endecott, to get revenge.

It is not known if the Narragansett living on Block Island had anything to do with Oldham's death. Pequot were believed to have hijacked the boat. This did not matter to Endecott's force. They burned a number of Narragansett villages on Block Island and then crossed over to Connecticut to search out any Pequot who had been involved. The colonists at Saybrook were very upset that the force from Massachusetts had been sent to deal with the Pequot. They feared that if the Pequot were attacked by Endecott and his men, they would suffer reprisals.

Endecott did not listen to the people of Saybrook and attacked several Pequot villages. They burned the villages and killed one Native American. Sassacus, the Pequot leader, did as the people of Saybrook feared and sought revenge. In the winter of 1636–37,

Sassacus and the Pequot attacked the fort at Saybrook and a number of smaller settlements. In spring 1637, the Pequot attacked Wethersfield and killed nine colonists.

The costs to the Pequot for these attacks were devastating. A large colonial army was gathered under the command of Captains John Underhill and John Mason of Connecticut. In addition to a large force of colonists, many Native Americans joined in. The colonists used the traditional rivalries among the Native American groups to recruit allies. Mohegan, Narragansett, and Niantic warriors fought alongside the colonists. On May 26, 1637,

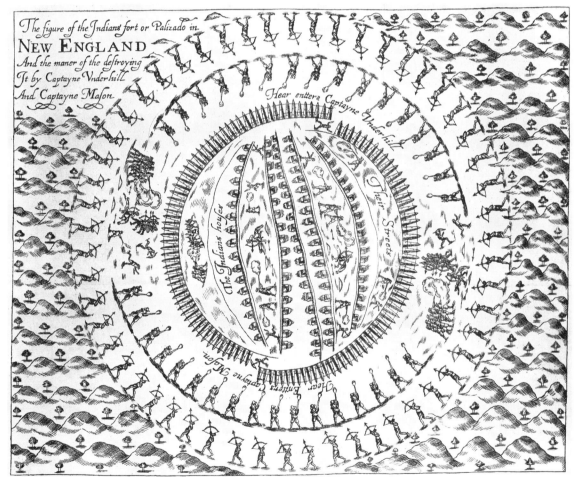

First published in a 1638 book, this illustration depicts the Pequot village that a colonial army led by Captains John Underhill and John Mason attacked in 1637. *(Library of Congress, Prints and Photographs Division [LC-USZ62-32055])*

Excerpt from John Underhill's *Account of the Pequot War*

Mercy they did deserve for their valour, could we have had opportunitie to have bestowed it; many were burnt in the Fort, both men, women, and children, others forced out, and came in troopes to the Indians, twentie, and thirtie at a time, which our souldiers received and entertained with the point of the sword; downe fell men, women, and children, those that scaped us, fell into the hands of the Indians, that were in the reere of us; it is reported by themselves, that there were about foure hundred soules in this Fort, and not above five of them escaped out of our hands. Great and dolefull was the bloudy sight to the view of young souldiers that never had beene in Warre, to see so many soules lie gasping on the ground so thicke in some places, that you could hardly passe along. It may bee demanded, Why should you be so furious (as some have said) should not Christians have more mercy and compassion? But I would referre you to Davids warre, when a people is growne to such a height of bloud, and sinne against God and man, and all confederates in the action, there hee hath no respect to persons, but harrowes them, and sawes them, and puts them to the sword, and the most terriblest death that may bee: sometimes the Scripture declareth women and children must perish with their parents; some time the case alters: but we will not dispute it now. We had sufficient light from the word of God for our proceedings . . .

the combined forces attacked Sassacus's village at what is today Mystic, Connecticut. At first, the Pequot were able to repel their attackers from behind their palisades. However, the colonists and their allies set the village on fire. The Pequot who tried to escape were killed, those who stayed behind died in the flames. Somewhere between 500 and 1,000 Pequot, mostly women, children, and old men, died during the battle.

Sassacus and many of his warriors had fled. They were found in July in a swamp west of New Haven and were attacked again. This time, when Sassacus escaped, he fled to the territory of the Mohawk. The Mohawk did not want to appear to be on Sassacus's side. They beheaded him and let the colonists know they would no longer have to fear the Pequot leader.

The Pequot who survived were rounded up and became slaves. The colonists gave some of the Pequot to their Native American allies as payment for their help. Other Pequot were sold in the slave markets of the Caribbean. A few Pequot avoided capture and escaped. These Pequot joined the tribes that were willing to take them in. The colonists had effectively wiped out most of the

Atrocities against Native Americans

From the earliest explorers who kidnapped Native Americans through the Seven Years' War, which ended in 1763, the people of New England and the other colonies treated the people they found already living there terribly. The early explorers often kidnapped Native Americans to bring them back to England as novelties and curiosities to be displayed and/or sold into slavery. In other cases, Native Americans were intentionally given blankets and clothing that had been used by sick and/or dying colonists in hopes of infecting them with diseases that were often fatal.

People of European descent who felt that Native Americans should be treated justly, such as Roger Williams, were cast out of the Puritan communities. In battles between the colonists and Native Americans, the colonists often slaughtered women and children when they captured a village. When they did not murder their

(continues)

With the help of a few other families also in search of religious freedom, Roger Williams established Providence Colony (present-day Rhode Island) on land that he acquired from the Narragansett Indians. *(Library of Congress, Prints and Photographs Division [LC-USZ62-15057])*

(continued)

captives, the colonists would often sell the Native Americans as slaves to the plantation owners in the Caribbean.

The attitudes of the Puritans set the stage for the annihilation of Native Americans throughout the 17th, 18th, and 19th centuries. Even today, more than 100 years after the last armed conflict of the Indian wars, Native Americans often do not have the same opportunities as non-Indian Americans. The vast majority of Native Americans live on isolated reservations where the schools, housing, and other services are substandard. Despite the many accomplishments of the Puritans and others in the English colonies, their treatment of Native Americans was deplorable.

Pequot and stopped the use of Pequot tribal and place-names. Almost 20 years later, in 1655, the colonists freed the remaining Pequot slaves in New England and allowed them to return to the site of their village on the Mystic River.

The way the colonists dealt with the Pequot was very upsetting to many of the other Native Americans in New England. Many Pequot had been slaughtered by the colonists even as they were trying to surrender. After the Pequot War, the Native Americans of New England were wary of the colonists who kept arriving in larger and larger numbers each year.

THE NEW ENGLAND CONFEDERATION

By 1643, there were a number of English colonies in New England, each with its own government. Massachusetts was the largest, but Plymouth was still a separate colony. Connecticut and Rhode Island had been established along with a colony at New Haven that later became part of Connecticut. All these colonies shared concerns about conflicts with their Native American neighbors.

The colonies needed more and more land to support their fast growing populations. Sometimes, treaties were made where Native Americans were paid for the loss of their land. However, much of the time colonists would just take any land that they wanted. Realizing that additional conflicts were likely, the leaders of the New England colonies decided to form an alliance for their protection.

The colonies agreed to help defend each other and formed the New England Confederation. Although the confederation lasted for more than 40 years, there was often rivalry among the colonies. The leaders of Massachusetts thought they should have more of a say because their colony was by far the largest. The others thought each colony should be represented equally. This is an argument that would continue in one way or another until the U.S. Constitution was adopted.

The New England Confederation clearly recognized the independence of all its members in the running of their colonies. What they agreed to do was help each other in military matters. In 1675, the New England Confederation was put to its most serious test.

KING PHILIP'S WAR

By 1670, there were more than 50,000 white people in New England where 50 years earlier there had been none. Their settlements stretched out along the coast from what is now Maine to the border between Connecticut and New York. In Connecticut, colonists had moved up the Connecticut River valley into western Massachusetts. This rapid population growth created a great deal of tension in New England.

Primary among these tensions was the need for land. The Native Americans who inhabited the land before the English came obviously had first claim to it. However, England claimed the whole area as part of its empire. This was also complicated by border disputes between the four colonies of Massachusetts, Plymouth, Rhode Island, and Connecticut. Along the frontiers of the colonies, settlers often just took what they wanted and defended it as best they could.

In addition to the colonists' greed for more and more of the lands claimed by the various tribes in New England, there was an underlying racial intolerance on the part of the English colonists. Even Native Americans who had been converted to Christianity, called "Praying Indians" at the time, who fought alongside the colonists were treated as inferior citizens.

King Philip's War was the unavoidable outcome of this conflict between cultures and races. Metacom, also called Metacomet, or King Philip as the English called him, was the leader of the Wampanoag. He was the second son of Massasoit, the Wampanoag

Metacom, or King Philip, became chief of the Wampanoag in 1662. *(Library of Congress, Prints and Photographs Division [LC-USZ62-96234])*

leader who had befriended and helped the Pilgrims at Plymouth. His story and the account of the rebellion he led against the white colonists of New England show the roots of the mistreatment of Native Americans that continues to this day.

Unlike Massasoit, his sons saw the colonists as a threat on many levels. The whites continued to take Wampanoag land and fought amongst themselves over who had the right to control the sale of Native American lands. After Massasoit died, his eldest son, Wamsutta, became the leader, or sachem, of the Wampanoag. As the leader of the tribe, he negotiated land sales to Rhode Island. Under the leadership of Roger Williams, Rhode Island probably had the best relationship with its Native American neighbors of all the colonies.

The leaders of Plymouth Colony did not want to see Rhode Island gain any more land, especially where it encroached on lands that they claimed. Plymouth sent out a small force of men led by Major Josiah Wilson to get Wamsutta and bring him to Plymouth, where they planned to convince him that he had to sell land only to them. During his captivity in Plymouth, Wamsutta became sick, and he died on his way home.

On the death of Wamsutta, Metacom became the leader of the Wampanoag. He was angered over the death of his brother, believing that Wamsutta had been poisoned by his captors. Metacom entered into a plot to drive the colonists back into the sea from which they came. He sent representatives to tribes throughout the area hoping to build a coalition of Native Americans. In January 1675, rumors of a Native American uprising became believable for the colonists when a "Praying Indian" named John Sassamon reported to the governor of Plymouth Colony, Josiah Winslow, that Metacom was preparing for war.

Originally published in *Harper's New Monthly Magazine* in 1857 and quite partial to the colonists involved in the incident, this illustration depicts Native Americans attacking colonists in Tiverton, Rhode Island, during King Philip's War. The war's early phase included many attacks on similar small settlements. (*Library of Congress, Prints and Photographs Division [LC-USZ62-97114]*)

After reporting to Governor Winslow, John Sassamon was murdered. Metacom denied having any part in the murder. However, three Native Americans were captured, charged with the crime, and executed. Throughout the remainder of winter 1675, Wampanoag, Pocumtuc, and Nipmuc warriors attacked small settlements throughout the colonies. The outlying settlements, especially those in western Massachusetts in the Connecticut River Valley, felt the brunt of the early stages of the war.

In the meantime, the colonies had forced the Narragansett to sign a treaty in which they agreed to turn over all Wampanoag who might seek refuge with the Narragansett. In December 1675, Governor Winslow led a large force into Narragansett territory to make sure they were not harboring any Wampanoag. Without further negotiation or proof that the Narragansett had violated the treaty, Winslow's forces began burning Narragansett villages. On December 19, 1675, Winslow reached the Narragansett's main village,

Published in *Harper's New Monthly Magazine* in 1857 and partial to the involved colonists, this engraving illustrates the colonists' defeat of a Narragansett village in the Great Swamp of Rhode Island in December 1675. *(Library of Congress, Prints and Photographs Division [LC-USZ62-97115])*

which sat on high ground in the middle of the Great Swamp, which is near the current town of West Kingston, Rhode Island.

Normally, this village was a well-defended spot with water all around it. However, the winter of 1675–76 had already been a cold one, and the colonists' forces were able to reach the village over the frozen swamp. It has been estimated that 300 Narragansett warriors and an equal number of women and children were killed on that day. There was no evidence then or now that the Narragansett were ever allied with Metacom. The guerilla warfare of the Native Americans was met with large forces of colonists and their "Praying Indian" allies killing any Native Americans they could find.

It soon became obvious that King Philip's War was going to be the end of any hopes of Native Americans hanging on to any power in New England. Metacom was betrayed and the colonists with their Native American allies trapped him in a swamp near

In this illustration, the colonists of Hadley, Massachusetts, rally to fight the nearby Algonquian nations. This skirmish was one of many fought during King Philip's War. *(Library of Congress, Prints and Photographs Division [LC-USZ62-75122])*

Treachery in New Hampshire
(1676)

The main fighting during King Philip's War was far from the four towns of New Hampshire. However, after the war, some of the Native Americans who had fought escaped and found shelter among the Pennacook along the Merrimack River in New Hampshire. In September 1676, Judge Richard Waldron of Dover, who frequently traded with the Native Americans of New Hampshire, invited the Pennacook and their guests to a meeting in Dover. Waldron had assembled a large force of colonists and suggested that the colonists and the Pennacook fight a mock battle.

The Pennacook trusted Judge Waldron and went along with his plan and fired their muskets in the air. After the weapons of the Native Americans were emptied, Waldron and the colonists aimed at their guests and forced them to surrender. The Pennacook were later released. However, 200 Native Americans who had fought in King Philip's War were taken captive. All but eight of them were sold into slavery. The remaining eight were believed to have killed innocent colonists in raids and were executed. The Pennacook vowed revenge.

New Hope, Rhode Island. When Metacom's body was finally found among the fallen, the colonial commander, Captain Church, ordered that Metacom be decapitated and the remainder of his body cut in quarters. The head was returned to Plymouth, where it was put on public display.

In the end, more than 5,000 Native Americans and more than 2,500 colonists died during King Philip's War. Many captured Native Americans were transported to the Caribbean and sold as slaves. It has been estimated that these numbers represented 40 percent of the Native Americans and 5 percent of the whites in New England at the time. If that is the case, then King Philip's War was the bloodiest ever fought by North Americans. From that point forward, the relations between colonists (later the United States) and Native Americans was one of sending in the military first and then making peace with the survivors if there were any. However, ending any possible threat to the colonies from Native Americans was not the end of the problems the colonies faced.

4

Revolution, Reform, and Restoration in England

The rule of Charles I was a time of many problems in England. In 1629, Charles dissolved the English Parliament when it refused to give him the resources he needed to fight a war with Scotland. There were many Puritans in Parliament, including John Winthrop. The Puritans also objected to Charles's plans for the Church of England. Many refer to this time as the Great Migration, when thousands of Puritan and non-Puritan English people fled the chaos in England for the American colonies.

Charles I recalled Parliament in 1640, only to dismiss it after just three weeks. Later that year, Charles I recalled Parliament again. This Parliament stayed in session for the next 13 years during one of the darkest times in modern English history. The Puritans in Parliament and throughout the country rose up against Charles I, and a civil war began in 1642.

Charles I ruled England, Ireland, and Scotland from 1625 until his execution in 1649. *(Library of Congress, Prints and Photographs Division [LC-USZ62-91613])*

This engraving, inspired by an early 17th-century derogatory verse by Richard Brathwaite, satirizes the Puritans' staunch beliefs. The illustration depicts a Puritan (far right) hanging his cat for killing a bird on Sunday, thereby not honoring what many believed should be a day of rest. *(Library of Congress, Prints and Photographs Division [LC-USZ62-30267])*

The Puritans in the English Civil War were called "Roundheads" because they wore their hair in a close-cropped fashion that was in keeping with the simple dress that the Puritans adopted. The king's followers wore their hair long and were referred to as "Cavaliers," a term that had been used in the past to describe mounted knights.

Oliver Cromwell rose to the top of the Puritan army and proved to be a very capable military leader. His "New Model Army" won a number of victories and eventually defeated the forces of the king. Charles I was tried and executed for treason on January 30, 1649. After defeating the Catholic and royalist forces in Ireland and Scotland, Oliver Cromwell became the Lord Protector of England. During the English Civil War, the colonies had been left alone and had developed ways of governing themselves. In Massachusetts and the four New Hampshire towns, the town meeting became the prominent form of government. The voting members of the community would gather and make decisions for the town. This is a practice that still exists in many small New England towns.

Oliver Cromwell was a Puritan and military leader who eventually became Lord Protector of England. *(Library of Congress, Prints and Photographs Division [LC-USZ62-95711])*

After the victory of the Puritans in England, there was a period of reverse migration, when large numbers of people went back to England to be a part of the Puritan country that was being created. Many leaders in New England were concerned that England would become the place of Puritan power and this would affect the way they lived and worshipped.

In England, Cromwell and his advisers saw that trade with the colonies in North America had suffered. Due to the turmoil of the

Voting Rights in New Hampshire

When the four towns of New Hampshire became part of Massachusetts, the strict laws of the Puritans, although not always enforced, became the law of the land. One exception was the rules that spelled out who could vote. In Massachusetts, only males who were members of Puritan churches were allowed to vote. In New Hampshire, voters did not have to be Puritans.

English Civil War and the disruption in trade that it caused, many traders in North America and especially those in Massachusetts had begun trading with the French and the Dutch in the Caribbean and Europe. To bring trade with the colonies back under control of England, Parliament passed the first Navigation Act in 1651. The part of this law that most affected the merchants of Boston and Portsmouth stated that colonies could only trade with England.

Many believe that the Navigation Act of 1651, as well as the additions to it over the next 40 years, had two consequences. First, some merchants continued to trade as they had in defiance of the English laws. Other merchants obeyed the law but felt that it was unfair. Although the importance of the Navigation Acts in eventually bringing about the American Revolution is probably minimal, they did contribute to a sense of defiance toward England.

Although Cromwell's victories were in part a victory for the rising middle classes in England, the country was not really ready

Excerpt from the Navigation Act of 1651

For the increase of the shipping and the encouragement of the navigation of this nation, which under the good providence and protection of God is so great a means of the welfare and safety of this Commonwealth: be it enacted by this present Parliament, and the authority thereof, that from and after the first day of December, one thousand six hundred fifty and one, and from thence forwards, no goods or commodities whatsoever of the growth, production or manufacture of Asia, Africa or America, or of any part thereof; or of any islands belonging to them, or which are described or laid down in the usual maps or cards of those places, as well of the English plantations as others, shall be imported or brought into this Commonwealth of England, or into Ireland, or any other lands, islands, plantations, or territories to this Commonwealth belonging, or in their possession, in any other ship or ships, vessel or vessels whatsoever, but only in such as do truly and without fraud belong only to the people of this Commonwealth, or the plantations thereof, as the proprietors or right owners thereof; and whereof the master and mariners are also for the most part of them of the people of this Commonwealth, under the penalty of the forfeiture and loss of all the goods that shall be imported contrary to this act; as also of the ship (with all her tackle, guns and apparel) in which the said goods or commodities shall be so brought in and imported; the one moiety to the use of the Commonwealth, and the other moiety to the use and behoof of any person or persons who shall seize the goods or commodities, and shall prosecute the same in any court of record within this Commonwealth.

Charles II
(1630–1685)

Charles II was 19 years old when his father was executed in 1649. Charles, his brother James, and many of his father's supporters were forced to leave England. Scotland and parts of Ireland recognized him as king, and in 1651 he invaded England from Scotland with an army of 10,000 soldiers. As Charles made his way south, people turned out to greet his army and proclaim him king. However, on September 3, 1651, Charles's army was defeated by Oliver Cromwell in a battle near the English town of Worcester.

Charles fled to France, where he lived in poverty until he returned as king after a royalist army defeated the Puritans. Before he could take the throne, he was forced to give more power to Parliament. Charles II ruled from 1660 until his death in 1685. During his reign, life in England was relatively calm; however, Charles was constantly in need of money to support his lavish lifestyle as king. He may have been trying to make up for the years he had lived in poverty in exile.

for the strict ideals of the Puritans. When Cromwell died in 1658, his son took over as Lord Protector. He lasted only nine months in the job before he resigned, and a battle began to restore Charles II, Charles I's son, to the throne.

After a number of battles, Charles II's forces prevailed and the monarchy was restored. Charles II ruled as king of England, Scotland, and Ireland for the next 25 years. At the restoration of the monarchy, many Puritans fled to the colonies. This was a period of relative stability in England, and the king and his ministers were able to devote some of their attention to the English colonies in North America. After years of benign neglect, Charles II wanted to reassert his control over what he saw as English territory.

The leaders of Massachusetts Bay Colony were very outspoken in their resistance to royal control. They believed that their charter

Charles II ruled England, Scotland, and Ireland from 1660 until his death in 1685. *(Library of Congress, Prints and Photographs Division [LC-USZ62-96910])*

The Heirs of John Mason

John Mason died unexpectedly in 1635 at the age of 49. His vast estates in Europe and New England were left to his grandchildren. At the time, the oldest grandchild was seven. Over the next 150 years, the heirs of John Mason filed 160 lawsuits in an attempt to get New Hampshire back. Although their claims were probably justified, they never were able to reclaim any of the property lost in New England.

gave them the right to run their own affairs. Charles II and his advisers tried to lessen the power of Massachusetts. First, they took away the lands to the north. In 1679, New Hampshire once again became a separate colony, this time with a royal charter. The new charter allowed for a president and council appointed by the king. It also provided for an assembly elected by the voters of New Hampshire. John Cutt became New Hampshire's president. Cutt and his two brothers, Robert and Richard, were wealthy merchants who owned ships and large tracts of land they had received from Massachusetts grants. John Cutt became active in royal politics, in part to protect his holdings out of fear that John Mason's heirs would have a better chance of reclaiming his properties in New Hampshire.

5

Royal Control of New Hampshire

Being a royal colony was good for New Hampshire. It allowed the four original towns to become separate from Massachusetts. With a resident of Portsmouth appointed governor and the council made up of local people from the towns, it seemed that New Hampshire would be governing itself within the framework of a royal charter. The 1680 Commission of John Cutt that created the Province of New Hampshire also established the border with Massachusetts. It said that New Hampshire included all lands, "lying & extending from three miles northward of the Merrimack River, or any part thereof to ye Province of Maine . . ."

Included within the boundaries of the Province of New Hampshire was a fifth town. In 1673, Massachusetts had granted a charter to the town of Dunstable that was located on the Merrimack River just after it turns north into New Hampshire. Dunstable's name was later changed to Nashua, and it was the first New Hampshire town that was not close to the ocean. Even with the addition of Dunstable, New Hampshire's population was just over 2,000 people in 1680. At the same time, the population of Massachusetts was almost 40,000.

ESTABLISHING A GOVERNMENT

Although the people of New Hampshire were not active participants in the government of Massachusetts, they had adopted the

Massachusetts form of town government. This allowed each community the ability to oversee its own local affairs. Town officials were elected on a yearly basis, and once a year, a town meeting was held where voters decided what was to happen in the town. This form of local government still exists in New Hampshire, and the second Tuesday in March is set aside as town meeting day throughout New Hampshire. With the experience of participating in town government, it was relatively easy for the people of the province to participate in the governing of all of New Hampshire.

Although the laws of England applied in royal colonies, colonial assemblies created laws as well. New Hampshire's assembly passed numerous laws to govern the conduct of the people in the province. They made laws that defined crimes such as murder, treason, and witchcraft. They also created laws that would seem a little strange today.

Shown in an engraving dated to about 1850, Nashua was the first New Hampshire town located away from the coast. *(New Hampshire Historical Society)*

Some Early Laws of New Hampshire

One law that might startle people today was written to deal with unruly children. It stated that a son who was 16 or older who refused to listen to his parents was to be brought before a magistrate, which is what they called the judges of the time. The magistrate was given the authority to "put to death or otherwise severely punish" the disobedient son.

Burglars were also treated harshly by the laws of New Hampshire. For the first offense, a "B" was to be branded, or burned, onto the right hand of the burglar. On the second offense, the left hand was branded. A third offense became a capital crime and the burglar could be put to death.

In addition to the laws that applied to criminals and misbehaving children, New Hampshire also passed a law that defined the voting rights of the people. To vote in the Province of New Hampshire, one had to be 24 years old, an Englishman, a Protestant, and have an estate worth at least £24. Although these rules limited the number of voters, they were more liberal than some of the other colonies that had higher monetary qualifications or required voters to belong to a specific church.

It appeared that the Province of New Hampshire was off to a good start. However, due to the amount of power that rested with the president of the province, the government was only as good as the person at the top of it. John Cutts's term in office was cut short by his death in 1681. Richard Waldron of Dover served briefly until a new royal appointee could be sent out from England. In November 1682, Edward Cranfield arrived from England in Portsmouth with the title of lieutenant governor.

Cranfield came to New Hampshire to increase his personal wealth and to validate the claims of the Mason heirs. Cranfield had purchased a share in those claims and was intent on taking back the land of New Hampshire that he considered his. First, he dissolved the assembly, and then court proceedings were held to legitimize the Mason claims. The courts charged the people large fees as a way of raising money for the governor. They also settled most cases in favor of the governor and the other people with Mason claims.

However, the people of New Hampshire were not going to lose their lands that easily. When lands were put up for auction to compensate the Mason claims, no one would bid on their neighbor's homes and farms. Outsmarted by the people, Cranfield decided to raise taxes to create more money for himself. Again, the people of New Hampshire refused to pay. When special tax collectors were sent out, they were met by angry residents of the towns. The governor's tax collectors were mistreated and came back without collecting any taxes.

Cranfield continued his campaign against the people of New Hampshire. Many were unjustly put in jail. The people of New Hampshire repeatedly complained to officials in London. Eventually, an investigation was begun. The Privy Council in London finally agreed with the people, and Cranfield was recalled in 1685. Although Cranfield was gone, New Hampshire's future was uncertain as a new king with new ideas for the colonies took over in London.

The Gove Rebellion

Edward Gove, a resident of Hampton who had been a member of the assembly, was so upset by Cranfield's behavior that he convinced a number of his neighbors to take action. On January 27, 1683, Gove and about a dozen people armed themselves and headed for Exeter. However, before they got very far, Nathaniel Weare, a justice of the peace in Hampton, organized a group who stopped Gove before he left town. Gove and his followers were convinced to lay down their weapons.

Cranfield saw this as an opportunity to show the people he was in charge. Gove was arrested and indicted on February 1, 1683, for high treason. He was convicted and told his sentence would be "hanged by the neck, and cut down alive; your entrails shall be taken out and burned before your face, your head cut off, and your body divided into four quarters; and your head and quarters be disposed of at the king's pleasure." Fortunately, Cranfield's commission prohibited him from using capital punishment.

Gove was sent to England where he was held in the Tower of London. Eventually, his family and friends were able to get his sentence reduced. He was pardoned by King James II in 1685 and allowed to return to New Hampshire, where his property was returned to him.

DOMINION OF NEW ENGLAND

After 25 years with Charles II as king, his brother, James II, a Catholic, became king of England in 1685. James's religion created all sorts of conflicts for him. He was king for only four years before he was overthrown. In that short time, he created havoc in the colonies as well as in England. In 1686, he consolidated the New England colonies of Massachusetts, Maine, New Hampshire, Plymouth, and Rhode Island into one colony called the Dominion of New England.

The first president of the dominion was Joseph Dudley, a Boston merchant. He was soon replaced when, in December 1686, Sir Edmund Andros arrived in Boston to take up his post as royal governor of the Dominion of New England. By 1688, the Dominion of New England had been expanded to include all of New England, from Nova Scotia to the north, and New York and New Jersey to the south. Part of the justification for the dominion was the growing conflict between the English colonies and the French colony in Canada. However, Andros ruled the dominion as a dictator, backed up by troops he had brought from England.

Andros suspended the colonial governments and set up his own courts. Town meetings were still allowed but could only meet once a year. Andros also levied taxes on the colonies without the consent of the colonists. In addition, he forced religious tolerance on the colonies and favored the Church of England over the Puritan churches.

When it was learned that James II had been overthrown in a bloodless rebellion referred to as the Glorious Revolution, the colonists seized this as their opportunity to oust Andros. Andros had been on a military expedition in the spring of 1689 to the frontier to defend the colonies against raids by Native Americans allied with the French

Joseph Dudley governed Massachusetts and New Hampshire from 1702 until 1715. *(Library of Congress, Prints and Photographs Division [LC-USZ62-120400])*

James, Duke of York and Albany, Later King James II
(1633–1701)

In 1649, King Charles I was removed from the throne and executed after a Puritan revolution in England. His two sons, Charles, prince of Wales, and James, duke of York and Albany, were forced to spend the next eight years living in exile while the Puritan Oliver Cromwell ran England. Charles lived in poverty in the Netherlands, and James went to Spain, where he joined the Spanish navy in its war against Protestant England. When the English monarchy was restored in 1660, James's older brother became Charles II, king of England.

Charles II appointed James lord high admiral of the navy and in 1664 granted James all the lands between the Connecticut and Delaware Rivers in North America. James sent a fleet to capture the territory claimed by the Dutch and was involved with the fate of New York and New Jersey for the next 24 years.

In 1672, James created a controversy by revealing that he had converted to Catholicism. Although England tolerated many different Protestant sects, the country was not tolerant of Catholics. In fact, in 1673, Parliament passed a series of laws called the Tests Acts, which barred Catholics from holding office. James was forced to resign his position as lord high admiral.

Because his brother had not produced an heir, James was next in line to become king of England. On his brother's death in 1685, many tried to block James from becoming king. However, they were unsuccessful, and he became James II, king of England.

As king, he was faced with a number of uprisings in England. He was extremely brutal in addressing any resistance to his rule. He was so unpopular that, in 1688, he was removed from the throne in a bloodless coup known as the Glorious Revolution. After a brief and unsuccessful attempt to regain his throne, he spent the rest of his life living in exile in France.

James II, as shown in this early 19th-century engraving, ruled England for only four years—1685 to 1688. *(Library of Congress, Prints and Photographs Division [LC-USZ62-92123])*

Dominion of New England, 1686–1689

NEW FRANCE

St. Lawrence R.

Lake
Ontario

Maine
(part of Mass.)

Hudson R.

Connecticut R.

New York

Massachusetts

Boston ● *Massachusetts Bay*

Connecticut

Plymouth

Rhode Island

Pennsylvania

Delaware R.

New York

East Jersey

Philadelphia ●

West Jersey

Maryland

Delaware

ATLANTIC OCEAN

N

Virginia

Dominion of New England

Other British colonies

0		100 miles
0		100 km

James II made New Hampshire a part of the Dominion of New England to consolidate his control over the colonies. The Dominion ended when James II was dethroned during the Glorious Revolution.

This illustration shows William III, prince of Orange, at the 1690 Battle of the Boyne in which his Protestant forces defeated James II's Catholic forces.
(Library of Congress, Prints and Photographs Division [LC-USZ62-54812])

in Canada. When he got back to Boston, the local population was in rebellion. A group had been formed and called itself the Committee for the Safety of the People. On April 18, 1689, Sir Edmund Andros was arrested and put in Boston's jail by members of the committee. Elsewhere in the dominion, Andros's appointed leaders were also removed from office. Shortly thereafter, Andros and his staff were sent back to England, and the Dominion of New England ended.

In the early days of the American Revolution, many colonists looked back at the overthrow of Edmund Andros as the first act in the long struggle for independence. This may be the case, but the changes affected by enforced religious tolerance and the rule of a royal governor greatly lessened the powers of the Puritan leaders of Massachusetts and left New Hampshire in a state of confusion.

THE FATE OF NEW HAMPSHIRE

The people in New Hampshire were torn in two directions. Many wanted to rejoin Massachusetts. Others wanted New Hampshire to remain a separate colony. Those in favor of becoming part of Massachusetts circulated a petition and got more than 350 signatures. The petition was sent to Boston and in March 1690 was accepted by the leaders there who were happy to have the towns of New Hampshire back. However, many of the people in New Hampshire were not pleased

Edmund Andros ruled the Dominion of New England as its royal governor. *(Published by George Burner, 1903)*

with the petition and the quick action by Massachusetts. They refused to pay any taxes that were to go to Massachusetts. Others did not know whose laws to follow.

In London, the new king, William, was as concerned with the growing power of Massachusetts as his predecessors had been. When it came time to issue a new charter to the colony, his councilors made sure that New Hampshire did not become part of Massachusetts, although they did allow Massachusetts to hang on to Maine. During this time, New Hampshire continued to grow slowly in population. However, many in the colony were experiencing a certain amount of success.

Trade had become very important. The merchants of Portsmouth were shipping lumber and masts to England as the Royal Navy prepared for war with France. At the same time, a lucrative trade was established with the islands of the Caribbean.

The fishermen of New Hampshire supplied large amounts of dried and salted fish that were used to feed the slaves of the sugar plantations in the islands. Lumber was also traded in the Caribbean, as most of the usable lumber on the islands had already been cut down. In spite of laws prohibiting it, some of this trade was with the French islands. England and France were at war, and that war soon spilled over into New Hampshire and the rest of the colonies that were bordered by New France (Canada).

6

War, Wood, and Wentworths

France and Britain were rivals around the world as each country tried to become the dominant power. Between 1689 and 1763, the two countries went to war four times, and in North America they are called the French and Indian wars. During all four of these wars, fighting took place between the French and their Native American allies and the English colonies in North America. New Hampshire was relatively close to the French settlements along the Saint Lawrence River and was frequently attacked by Native Americans who were supplied and encouraged by the French. Most of these attacks were by the Abenaki, who had lost land in New Hampshire and Maine. The first two of these wars played a major part in the lack of population growth of the New Hampshire colony.

KING WILLIAM'S WAR
1689–1697

In Europe, the first of these wars between France and Britain was called the War of the League of Augsburg. The colonists in North America simply referred to it as King William's War. In New Hampshire, the very existence of the colony was threatened by this war. The Pennacook, who were still angry about Richard Waldron and the trickery he used to capture their guests in 1676, used the outbreak of war to gain their revenge.

William III, prince of Orange, ruled England, Scotland, and Ireland jointly with Mary II from 1689 until Mary's death in 1694. Afterward, William III ruled alone until 1702. *(Library of Congress, Prints and Photographs Division [LC-USZC2-2734])*

In June 1689, the people of New Hampshire were so worried about attacks by Native Americans that they had taken to sleeping in garrisoned or fortified houses. In Dover, five of the houses had walls built around them. All the people of the town spent their nights in one of the garrisoned houses where they could defend themselves. On the night of June 27, a few Native American women came to Dover and said they would be followed the next day by members of their tribe who wished to come and trade. The women asked for shelter for the night.

Waldron felt that the defenses in Dover were such that there was no need for concern and invited the women to spend the night inside the garrisons. No guards were posted, and during the night the women sneaked out and opened the gates for a large force of Abenaki warriors. Although there are conflicting reports, somewhere between 20 and 50 colonists were killed in the raid. Richard Waldron was tied to a chair and tortured before he was finally forced to fall on his own sword and die.

In addition to the people killed, many others were taken prisoner and marched north. Some were later released. Others died in captivity or along the way. One group that was taken was not given any food for three weeks, and they were forced to eat bark and other plant material to stay alive. During this period, many people abandoned their outlying farms and moved into Portsmouth. When people worked in their fields or in the woods cutting trees, they needed to post guards to prevent ambushes.

As the war progressed, there were atrocities on both sides. Many were forced to join the militia to fight against the French-supplied Native Americans. The pay in the militia was very low, but the soldiers were paid a bounty for the scalps of Native Americans they killed, including women and children. One group of militia came upon a group of warriors at night in the woods and attacked and killed them in their sleep.

Hannah Dustin
(1657–1736)

On March 15, 1697, Native Americans attacked the town of Haverhill, Massachusetts, on the Merrimack River on the border of New Hampshire. They killed around 30 people and took a number of captives. Among those captured were Hannah Dustin, her baby, and the baby's nurse, Mary Neff. The warriors headed north up the valley of the Merrimack River in their canoes with their captives and soon killed the Dustin baby. The group traveled almost 100 miles upriver over several days and were camped on an island in the river near modern-day Concord, New Hampshire.

At this point, there were 10 warriors and a Native American woman and child escorting the prisoners. During the night, Dustin, Neff, and a boy named Samuel Leonardson, who had also been captured, decided to make their escape. But Dustin was not leaving without exacting revenge for her lost child. She and her two fellow captives took hatchets from the sleeping warriors and killed all 10 of them, sparing only the woman and child. After killing the warriors, the two English women and the boy scalped them. They then took one of the Native American canoes and went back down the river to Haverhill.

Throughout King William's War, the people in New Hampshire lived in fear of attack. Even when Native Americans were not involved, the war disrupted the economy of New Hampshire. The profitable fishing industry that was based on the Isles of Shoals and many of the islands off the Maine coast was abandoned because there was no way to defend the fishermen against French naval attack. Between 1690 and 1700, the population of New Hampshire increased by fewer than 800 people, and there were still fewer than 5,000 people in the whole colony. It was not until after the next war that New Hampshire saw any substantial growth in population.

QUEEN ANNE'S WAR
1702–1713

After just four short years of peace, fighting broke out again between France and Britain. This time, the war in Europe was over who would become the next king of Spain. The next in line for the

Spanish throne was a relative of the king of France. Many were concerned he would eventually become the king of France as well, and the rest of Europe feared the joining of the two countries under one king. For that reason, the conflict is known as the War of the Spanish Succession. The English colonists in North America were little concerned with the politics in Europe and called this phase of the fight for control of North America Queen Anne's War, after their new ruler.

For New Hampshire, Queen Anne's War must have seemed like a continuation of the previous war. The outlying towns of Hampton and Exeter were repeatedly attacked by Native Americans. Many of the attacks that took place in New Hampshire and Maine were by Native Americans living in Norridgewock, Maine. A Catholic priest had set up a mission there and converted many of the Western Abenaki. Pennacook and other Western Abenaki from New Hampshire joined the people in Norridgewock.

The wars in North America were about control of the continent, but they also pitted Catholics against Protestants. Catholic priests were an important part of the colonizing effort in New France. Native Americans were converted to Catholicism and told that killing Protestants was good. The priest in Norridgewock was especially effective at both conversion and at inciting his parishioners to attack the English settlements in Maine, New Hampshire, and over the border into Massachusetts.

Most of New Hampshire had suffered during the nearly 25 years of continuous warfare. There had been hundreds of people killed on both sides, and the colonists went forward with a deep hatred of those Native

Daughter of James II, Queen Anne ruled Great Britain (the newly United Kingdom of England and Scotland) and Ireland from 1702 until her death in 1714. This engraving is from a statue of the leader at Blenheim Palace in Woodstock, England. *(Library of Congress, Prints and Photographs Division [LC-USZ62-110255])*

Father Sébastien Rasle
(ca. 1654–1724)

Father Rasle came to Canada as a missionary in 1689 and at first worked with Native Americans near Quebec. In 1693, he moved his mission to Norridgewock on the Kennebec River in Maine. It was in Norridgewock that he became the scourge of northern New England. Rasle is reported to have had a flag that had a cross on it that was surrounded by bows and arrows. Entire tribes came to Norridgewock and converted.

The colonists tried a number of times to put an end to Father Rasle and his followers. Attacks in 1705 and 1721 burned the church and many of the surrounding buildings, but the English were unable to catch Father Rasle. Finally, in 1724, a force of 200 Englishmen came up the Kennebec River in 17 whale boats. This time, they caught Rasle. When the leader of the attack, Lieutenant Richard Jacques, asked Rasle to surrender, the priest refused. Jacques then shot him in the head. Eighty of Rasle's followers were killed and scalped. When the colonists went through Rasle's possessions, they found letters from French officials encouraging him to use his followers to fight the English colonists.

Americans still in the Northeast. Portsmouth was the only area of the colony that experienced any expansion or prosperity during these first two wars. A large part of Portsmouth's success came from the trade in timber products and shipbuilding.

THE TREES OF NEW HAMPSHIRE

The wars between France and Britain were fought in Europe, the Americas, and elsewhere around the world. To fight in so many places required an ever growing navy, and that navy needed large amounts of timber, especially trees large enough to be used as masts. By the 17th and 18th centuries, most of the forests of Europe had been cut down. The British turned to the colonies in North America for suitable wood for their ships. The supply of wood for shipbuilding was so important that a surveyor general of the King's Woods was appointed to encourage the timber industry in the colonies.

In New Hampshire, during the wars, many farmers and other residents of the colony spent at least part of the year working in the woods. The most valuable trees were huge white pines that could be used for masts, yardarms, and spars. The pines grew straight and tall, and crews would travel deep into the forests to find and harvest them. Harvesting crews were accompanied by groups of guards to protect them from ambush. This procedure of having armed guards worked so well that only twice during the wars were people working in the woods successfully attacked by Native Americans.

Colonists in New Hampshire harvested the eastern white pine for many purposes, primarily to use as ship masts. *(Facts On File, Inc.)*

In addition to the people who worked in the woods, there were numerous sawmills and other finishing factories for the trees harvested in New Hampshire's forests. The trade in masts was so lucrative that a merchant buying masts and spars in Portsmouth could earn four or five times his investment when they were sold in England. New Hampshire was producing so much marine timber that trade was also conducted with other countries in Europe, and special "mast ships" were built just to carry the huge pine logs that had been fashioned into masts.

The forests of New Hampshire also supplied wood for local shipbuilders. All manner of boats and ships were built in Portsmouth. They even built some warships for the British navy. Later, at the time of the Revolutionary War, New Hampshire shipbuilders built ships to be used in the fight for independence.

THE WENTWORTHS

The Wentworths were one of the most powerful and influential families in the colonial history of New Hampshire. With the exception of one 10-year period, one of three Wentworths was the head of New Hampshire from 1717 to 1775. All these Wentworths were wealthy Portsmouth merchants. For much of this time, they ran New Hampshire as if it was their personal kingdom.

John Wentworth became lieutenant governor in 1717, when New Hampshire was overseen by the royal governor in Massachusetts. As lieutenant governor for New Hampshire, he used his position to fill the council with his friends and relatives. He also appointed people who supported his rule to positions throughout the colony. During the 13 years that he was in power, he worked behind the scenes to further separate New Hampshire from Massachusetts. It was through his planning and the efforts of the colony's agents in London that

During his tenure as lieutenant governor, John Wentworth strove for New Hampshire's independence from Massachusetts. This copy of a portrait painted in 1760 (30 years after Wentworth's death) imagines him in 1760s fashions. *(Public Archives of Nova Scotia)*

Son of John Wentworth, Benning Wentworth became the first royal governor of New Hampshire in 1741. This 1760 painting shows Wentworth with added padding to emphasize his wealth. *(Collections of the State of New Hampshire Division of Historical Resources)*

the border dispute with Massachusetts was finally settled.

John Wentworth died in 1730, and for the next 10 years there was a certain amount of political chaos in New Hampshire. When the Crown finally established the new boundaries for New Hampshire, a Wentworth was made the first independent royal governor of New Hampshire. In 1741, Benning Wentworth, the oldest of John Wentworth's 16 children, became the leader of New Hampshire.

Benning Wentworth remained governor until 1767, which was the longest tenure in office of any British governor in America. During that time, he ruled New Hampshire in such a way that the majority of people supported him. He also made sure that he and his close associates and family members amassed great wealth. Those who benefited most during the governorship of Benning Wentworth did so in two primary ways.

As governor, Wentworth was responsible for granting land in the colony. During his time in office, Benning Wentworth made grants for more than 200 townships in New Hampshire and west of the Connecticut River, which was called the New Hampshire Grants at the time. This area later became Vermont and was also claimed by New York. Wentworth granted land to anyone who had the money, but he required that members of his family and associates be included as proprietors of the grant. He also reserved 500 to 800 acres of land for himself within each grant.

The other direct benefit from being governor was being able to control the timber industry. The Crown had imposed strict rules to preserve the supply of suitable mast timber for the navy. It was up to the governor as the king's surveyor to ensure that these rules were followed. In his report to London, Benning Wentworth made sure he demonstrated that people in the lumber industry in New Hampshire were respecting the Crown's rules. The reality was far from the reported truth.

The governor allowed his merchant relatives and the colony's lumbermen to do whatever was needed in the forests of New Hampshire to ensure that there were plenty of profits, especially since the governor expected and got his share in the form of bribes and kickbacks. Rather than be upset by this, many of the people in the colony realized that what was good for the Wentworths was usually good for everyone else as well. Besides the prosperity created by the timber industry and the growth of the colony through the numerous land grants, Governor Wentworth worked to keep the general population satisfied by working closely with the assembly to improve the situation in the colony.

After 25 years of using the governorship to line his own pockets, the people of New Hampshire became upset with the governor, and he was forced to resign. It has been suggested that the governor's personal life may have also been responsible for forcing him out of office. When he was 64 years old, his wife died and he quickly married a young woman who had been a maid at his house. Many of the conservative people of the colony found this

Summer Houses

Today, New Hampshire is known as a mecca for tourists. Large numbers of people come in the winter to ski and enjoy other winter activities. In the summer, the numerous lakes of the state are packed with vacationers escaping the crowded and hot cities of Massachusetts and the states to the south. One of the first summer homes built in the colonies was built by Benning Wentworth. He had built an estate on Lake Wentworth, which is just east of Lake Winnipesaukee.

John Wentworth II also built a summer home on the lakes at Wolfeboro on Lake Winnipesaukee. His summer estate consisted of 6,000 acres with a house that measured 102 feet long by 41 feet wide. In addition to the main house there were numerous outbuildings and barns. These included shops for the resident blacksmith, carpenter, and cabinetmaker. Some who saw Wentworth's summer home with its 600-acre park compared it to the great estates of Virginia, like George Washington's Mount Vernon.

Dartmouth College

In 1754, Dr. Eleazar Wheelock began a school for Native Americans in Lebanon, Connecticut. Over time, the school grew and began to accept white students as well as Native Americans. As Connecticut grew, the school needed to find a new location and looked to the north. Money was raised in England and Scotland for the school, and £10,000 was put into a trust headed by the earl of Dartmouth.

A number of potential sites for the school were considered. Five hundred acres that had belonged to Benning Wentworth in Hanover, New Hampshire, was finally selected for the school. Governor John Wentworth was instrumental in bringing the school to New Hampshire and gave the school a large grant of land in the northern reaches of the colony to support it. In 1770, Wheelock's Indian school reopened as Dartmouth College. The first year, there were 28 students. Ten of them were Native Americans, and the rest were white.

A lithograph published around 1834 shows, from left to right, Wentworth Hall, Dartmouth Hall, and Thornton Hall on the Dartmouth College campus. The oldest building on the campus, Dartmouth Hall was the only campus building until the 1820s. *(Library of Congress, Prints and Photographs Division [LC-USZ62-3924])*

much more outrageous than the graft and corruption that had marked his term as governor.

In 1767, Governor Benning Wentworth resigned. His nephew, John Wentworth II, became governor and was New Hampshire's final royal governor. He served until he fled the colony in 1775, fearing for his life and the lives of his family. During his time in office, John Wentworth II followed the practices of his grandfather and uncle. He continued to make land grants and worked for the network of Wentworth family and supporters. Had he not been a staunch Loyalist, he might have been able to continue as governor of the colony, and then the state, for a long time. He was respected for taking care of the people as well as his friends and family.

7

Growth, Forts, and More Wars

GROWTH OF THE COLONY

During the first century of New Hampshire's existence, the colony grew very slowly in comparison to other colonies. But that changed in the 37 years of relative peace that followed Queen Anne's War. In that time, the population of New Hampshire more than quadrupled. It went from just over 5,500 people in 1710 to more than 23,000 in 1740. Settlement during this time expanded into other areas of the colony as well, dividing the state into three geographical areas. There were the towns along the coast and bays near Portsmouth, the towns that followed Nashua up along the Merrimack River, and four new settlements along the Connecticut River.

During this time, there continued to be conflicts between New Hampshire and Massachusetts over which colony had the right to settle specific areas. Massachusetts made a number of land grants in what was actually New Hampshire. One of these grants was to a group of Scots-Irish immigrants who founded the town of Londonderry, New Hampshire.

During the religious upheavals of the 1700s in Britain, a large group of Scottish Presbyterians left Scotland for Northern Ireland where they hoped to be able to practice their religion in peace. Although they were granted religious freedom, many of these people resented the fact that they still had to pay taxes that supported the state-sponsored Anglican Church. They were also unhappy

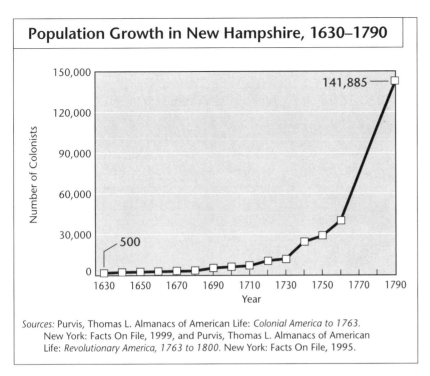

Population Growth in New Hampshire, 1630–1790

141,885

500

Number of Colonists

Year

Sources: Purvis, Thomas L. Almanacs of American Life: *Colonial America to 1763.*
New York: Facts On File, 1999, and Purvis, Thomas L. Almanacs of American
Life: *Revolutionary America, 1763 to 1800.* New York: Facts On File, 1995.

The population of New Hampshire grew slowly for many years. New Hampshire remained and continues to be one of the less populated states.

because there was no land in Ireland that they could own, and they were forced to be tenant farmers.

A large number of Scots-Irish people decided to move as a group to New England. On August 4, 1718, more than 100 families arrived in Boston and 20 other families arrived in Portland, Maine, which was part of Massachusetts at the time. They asked the government of Massachusetts for a place to start a community and were told they could have six square miles of unsettled land anywhere east of Boston. After looking carefully around, they chose a spot northeast of Nashua along what they called the West-running Brook. Initially, 16 families settled there and were soon joined by many of their fellow Scots-Irish. They named their new community Londonderry, after the city in Northern Ireland where many of them had lived. Once they had established their community, many more families followed them to New Hampshire.

Shortly after they had established Londonderry, the leaders of the community realized they were in New Hampshire, and that

The Potato in North America

Numerous Native American plants were adopted by Europeans. One of those was the potato, which was developed by Native Americans living in the mountains of South America. When the potato was brought to Europe, its cultivation spread rapidly, and it became one of the major crops in Ireland. It was the failure of the potato crops in 19th-century Ireland that forced many Irish people to emigrate to the United States at that time. The Scots-Irish who settled in Londonderry, New Hampshire, are credited with bringing the potato to New England, where it remains an important crop, especially in northern Maine.

The Scots-Irish brought the potato to New England from Europe. It is still an important crop, featured in regional specialities such as hash and New England boiled dinner. *(Library of Congress, Prints and Photographs Division [LC-USF34-041862-D])*

their charter from Massachusetts was not valid. The government of New Hampshire was glad to have these new settlers, and the assembly voted to grant them the land they already inhabited. They were also able to buy another 10 square miles from John Wheelwright, whose family had a deed to a large tract of land in the area that they had received from the Nashua tribe in 1629.

RUMFORD

In its ongoing battle over control of the Merrimack River Valley, Massachusetts made other land grants in the area. In 1721, the General Court of Massachusetts decided to establish a town up the

Merrimack at Pennacook. This had been the home of the Penna-cook band of Western Abenaki who had fled to Norridgewock during the war years. A trading post had been established there in 1660, but there were no permanent settlers. The General Court chose 100 families to settle there. They moved north and called their town Rumford.

To try and counter the move by Massachusetts to gain land claimed by New Hampshire, the New Hampshire assembly made a similar grant of land that they called Bow and offered it to some of the people in Londonderry. The dispute between the two colonies grew heated, and they eventually turned to London to settle their boundaries. Finally, in 1741, the king and his council came to a decision, and the southern boundary of New Hampshire was redefined. The established line, three miles north of the Merrimack River, was to stand until it reached a point due north of Pawtucket Falls. There the boundary would turn and run due west until it reached the colony of New York. This is the border between Massachusetts and New Hampshire that continues to exist today.

Although the people of Rumford were upset by the decision, they were now officially in New Hampshire. In 1765, the name of their community was changed to Concord, and it became the capital of New Hampshire in 1784. The new boundary not only solved the jurisdiction of Rumford and the rest of the Merrimack River Valley, it also gave New Hampshire more land to the west than it expected. The forts along the Connecticut River that had been set up by Massachusetts also now found themselves in New Hampshire.

FORTS ONE, TWO, THREE, AND FOUR

In 1704, during Queen Anne's War, the Connecticut River Valley town of Deerfield, Massachusetts, was attacked by French and Native American fighters. Forty-four people were killed and more than 100 were taken north to Canada as prisoners. More than half the prisoners died on the trip north. As the population of the Connecticut River Valley in Massachusetts rebounded and then grew, Massachusetts decided to do something to help defend the area.

In 1735, the Massachusetts General Court set up four plantations along the Connecticut River to the north. Each plantation was sold to a proprietor who in exchange for the land was to build a fort and start a community. These settlements were simply referred

During Queen Anne's War, the French forces allied with Canadian Indians destroyed Deerfield, Massachusetts, on the night of February 29, 1704. The final attack on the town is dramatized in this engraving. *(Library of Congress)*

to by their numbers, which started with number one, running north, to number four. Fort Number Four played an important role in the next war between the French and the British, but not before it became part of New Hampshire.

When the boundary dispute between Massachusetts and New Hampshire was settled, the new border extended west beyond the Connecticut River to New York. Forts one through four would become the New Hampshire towns of Chesterfield, Westmoreland, Walpole, and Charlestown.

KING GEORGE'S WAR
1744–1748

In 1744, France and England once again went to war. This time it was called the War of the Austrian Succession in Europe and King George's War in North America. Most of this war was fought in

Europe, but on April 19, 1746, Fort Number Four was attacked by Native Americans allied with the French. Attacks continued throughout the summer months and the French-backed Native

The Battle of Louisbourg
(June 1745)

On the tip of Cape Breton, Nova Scotia, the French had built a large fort to help protect their ships entering the Saint Lawrence River. In 1745, Governor Shirley of Massachusetts and other leaders decided to try and capture the fort. They raised an army of 4,000 men and received naval support from the British navy. An attack was planned and executed, and on June 17, 1745, the fort at Louisbourg surrendered. A number of colonies had participated in the expedition, and New Hampshire had sent 400 militia. The capture of Louisbourg was considered a great victory for the colonial forces.

Under the command of William Pepperell, a volunteer militia with members from Massachusetts, Connecticut, and New Hampshire defeated the French at Louisbourg, Cape Breton Island.
(Library of Congress, Prints and Photographs Division [LC-USZ62-105732])

Americans burned the community's crops, killed or stole their livestock, and burned all the outlying buildings. Unable to put away any food for the winter, Fort Number Four was abandoned and many of the people returned to Massachusetts.

In March 1747, 30 men led by Captain Phineas Stevens headed north to re-establish Fort Number Four. Shortly after they arrived, on April 7, 1747, the fort was attacked by a large force of French and Native American soldiers. Despite being attacked by a much larger force, Captain Stevens and his men were able to hold the fort. Their victory was greeted as very good news throughout New England. Had Fort Number Four fallen, the communities to the south and east would likely have been attacked next.

THE SEVEN YEARS WAR, OR THE FRENCH AND INDIAN WAR 1754–1763

The fourth and final war between the French and the British in North America actually started over the attempt by France to expand its colony westward and south to surround and contain the

On July 8, 1758, the British attacked the French at Fort Carillon, later known as Fort Ticonderoga. The fort was considered important because of its location at the juncture of Lakes Champlain and George. Shown in a drawing looking north from below the fort (right center), one can see tents lightly penciled in to mark a military encampment. *(Library of Congress, Prints and Photographs Division [DRWG/US=Unattributed, no. 16])*

British colonies. The French built forts in the Ohio River Valley, established missions and trading posts along the Mississippi River, and set up a colony along the Gulf of Mexico near the mouth of the Mississippi River. The British government decided that there was room for only one colonial power in North America.

In the first three wars, the fighting in North America had been done primarily by the colonial militia. In the French and Indian War, both Britain and France sent troops to North America. Fighting took place from the Ohio River Valley, all along the frontier between the English colonies and New France, and eventually along the Saint Lawrence River. In the end, the colonial and British forces prevailed, and Canada became British territory.

Militia from New Hampshire joined with the British regulars in the fight against the French and their Native American allies. It was in this war that the British employed a new type of soldier. In European wars, the armies would line up and fight in the open. In North America, the Native Americans fought using other techniques, like ambush and surprise raids against villages. During the French and Indian War, the British recruited a group of fighters in New Hampshire that were to function as scouts and as a countermeasure to the type of fighting done by the Native Americans.

Robert Rogers led a group that became known as Rogers's Rangers in the fight against the French and their Native American allies in the French and Indian War. *(National Archives of Canada)*

Robert Rogers, the son of Scots-Irish parents, had served as a scout in the previous war and was an able woodsman and fighter. Rogers was put in charge of a company of fighters called Rangers by the British. They were soon known as Rogers's Rangers and were involved in numerous battles as well as being valuable scouts. The Rangers dressed as woodsmen and were able to fight in the woods just like their Native American enemies. One of their well known battles was fought in the spring of 1758. The Rangers attacked a group of Native Americans not realizing that they were greatly outnumbered. They ended up losing the battle, but it was remarkable because it was fought on snowshoes.

In the early years of the French and Indian War, it seemed that the French had the upper hand. However, as Britain put more and

Robert Rogers
(1731–1795)

Robert Rogers was born in Methuen, Massachusetts, in 1731. His parents were part of the group of Scots-Irish immigrants who settled in Londonderry. The family later moved to a remote farm near Rumford (Concord), New Hampshire, where Robert spent as much time as he could in the woods. At the age of 14 in summer 1746, after a raid by Native Americans where five militiamen were killed, Rogers went with the group that pursued the raiders. Although they did not catch the Native Americans, Rogers had found the path that would make him one of the most famous fighters in the colonies.

Rogers was not interested in being a farmer, but he found it hard to make a living in the woods. In 1755, he was arrested for being involved with a group that was printing and circulating counterfeit New Hampshire currency. He was given the choice of joining the British army or going to jail. He chose the military and recruited 50 other New Hampshire woodsmen to join his group. Rogers was appointed captain of the Rangers. Rogers's friend, John Stark, who would become famous in the Revolutionary War, served as Rogers's second in command.

The group soon became known as Rogers's Rangers and they fought in many battles in the Lake Champlain area as well as in Canada. The Native Americans learned to fear the Rangers, who were their equals in both fighting skills and brutality. The Rangers were an independent group and would only follow the orders of Rogers and his subordinates. During the war, their exploits were romanticized in the newspapers in the colonies and in Great Britain.

After the war, Rogers fell on hard times. He had used some of his own money to finance the Rangers and fell deeply into debt as a result. Rogers ended up spending several years in debtors' prison in London. When the Revolutionary War began, Rogers wanted to return to New Hampshire and fight for the colonies. Unfortunately, people in the colonies believed he was a British spy, and he was not allowed to join the American forces.

Rogers returned to North America once again as a ranger with the Queen's American Rangers. The group was defeated in the only battle they fought in during the Revolution. Rogers returned to England and died in a London boardinghouse in 1795 at the age of 63.

more resources into the campaign in North America, the tide turned. Eventually, with the help of colonial militias and special forces like Rogers's Rangers, the British forces penetrated to the very heart of New France along the St. Lawrence River. In 1759, as the British prepared to attack Quebec, Rogers's Rangers were given a special mission. The town of Saint Francis was home to a large number of Christian Native Americans. It was the base for many of the raids that were conducted against the frontiers of northern New England and New York. Rogers and 200 of his Rangers were sent to destroy the town.

Just before dawn on October 2, 1759, the Rangers attacked. The people of the town never stood a chance and were wiped out. It is reported that the Rangers found more than 600 English scalps hanging in the village. The people of New England were much more excited by the destruction of St. Francis than they were by the capture of Quebec the same day. In 1760, the British mounted their final campaign against the French at Montreal. The capture of Montreal brought the fighting to an end in North America, but it was 1763 before the final terms were agreed to in the Treaty of Paris.

The colonies were now safe from the French and their Native American allies. However, the war had been very expensive and the British government was deeply in debt. They felt that since the colonies had benefited from the war, they should help pay for it. It was the attempt to tax the colonies over the next 12 years that brought about war between the colonies and Britain.

8

The Road to Revolution

THE SUGAR ACT
1764

For a number of years, Parliament had been trying to regulate trade in the colonies. Smuggling and trading with Britain's enemies had become standard practice in Boston and other major ports. At the end of the French and Indian War, Parliament attempted to do two things. First, it wanted to strengthen the position of the Crown's customs agents in the colonies. It also needed to raise tax revenue to pay its war debts. Parliament's first attempt to do this was called the Sugar Act.

The Sugar Act was passed by Parliament on April 5, 1764, and addressed the trade problems in the colonies. Sugar from the Caribbean was a major source of trade. It was imported into the colonies, especially Boston, and distilled into rum. The rum was then sold in Europe and elsewhere. An early law had tried to tax the sugar trade. The tax had been so large that merchants had found ways to get around it by trading with non-British sugar producers or by not paying the tax. The Sugar Act tried to make sure that all molasses and sugar would be taxed no matter where it was produced. It also gave more power to the customs officers to search ships and seize cargos or the ships themselves.

The part of the act that created the most problems for the colonists was that customs cases were no longer held in local courts. It had been very hard for British officials to get convictions in courts where the jury was made up of the friends, neighbors, or even the employees of the merchants charged with customs violations. Under the Sugar Act, customs cases were to be tried in a special Vice Admiralty Court in Halifax, Nova Scotia. Although the Sugar Act was not popular, it applied to only a relatively small group of merchants and did not cause much protest from the colonists. It also failed to raise much money for the Crown, so more sources of revenue were needed.

THE STAMP ACT
1765

If there was one event that turned the feelings of the colonies against the British government, it was the Stamp Act of 1765. On the face of it, the Stamp Act must have seemed fairly reasonable to the members of Parliament who passed it. However, in the colonies, it was seen as an infringement on the rights of the people. The act required that many transactions that took place in the colonies have a stamped receipt to prove they were legitimate transactions. In addition, newspapers and other printed documents would have to carry a stamp. When the people in the colonies heard about the Stamp Act, they were quick to organize against it. One of the positions of the Stamp Act opponents was that they were being taxed without representation.

Nearby Boston was one of the centers of protest against the Stamp Act. The people of New Hampshire were also very concerned and organized their own chapters of the Sons of Liberty. Local people in all the colonies were appointed to take on the job of being stamp agents. In New Hampshire, George Meserve, who was visiting in England at the time, was appointed stamp

When affixed to goods, this stamp signified that a tax must be paid upon purchase. Many colonists felt that the British unfairly introduced these taxes when they implemented the Stamp Act in 1765, which affected goods ranging from business transactions to playing cards. *(Library of Congress, Prints and Photographs Division [LC-USZ61-539])*

Sons of Liberty

When the Stamp Act was passed by Parliament in 1765, people in the colonies formed groups in their communities to protest the act. One of the opponents of the Stamp Act in the House of Commons, Isaac Barré, called the protestors the "sons of liberty." Soon the name spread to the colonies, where it was readily adopted. It was the various Sons of Liberty groups that organized protests against the Stamp Act and later held "tea parties" in places like Boston, New Jersey, and South Carolina when the Tea Act was passed. The Sons of Liberty were also responsible for forming the Committees of Correspondence that kept the Patriots throughout the colonies up to date on what was going on. Their letters, which were passed between these local committees, are credited with bringing about the First Continental Congress.

Displeasure with the Stamp Act was expressed throughout the colonies after the act's passage in 1765. Here, colonists in New York protest. *(Library of Congress, Prints and Photographs Division [LC-USZ61-536])*

agent. When he arrived in Boston, he was amazed at how upset people were about the Stamp Act. When he got home to Portsmouth, he found that the Sons of Liberty had hung effigies of him all over town. Meserve resigned immediately rather than face the anger of his neighbors.

On the day the Stamp Act was to take effect, the ships in Portsmouth Harbor flew their flags at half-mast and the churches rang their bells to mourn the death of liberty. A coffin was carried through town that had "Liberty—Aged 145" written on it. "Miss Liberty" was put in a grave, but pulled back out when the protestors claimed that her heart was faint but still beating. No stamps were issued in New Hampshire or in any of the other colonies with the exception of Georgia. Parliament repealed the Stamp Act in March 1766, and the people of New Hampshire celebrated with fireworks and the ringing of church bells.

The Stamp Act did have one negative impact on New Hampshire. It pointed out the fact that Governor Wentworth, his council, and many of the assembly members did not share the feelings of the people. When the other colonies called for a Stamp Act Congress in October 1765 to present a united response to the Crown, Wentworth and his followers in the government refused to send delegates. After receiving substantial pressure from the people of New Hampshire, the colony did approve the report put out by the Stamp Act Congress known as the Resolutions of the Continental Congress.

Excerpt from the Resolutions of the Continental Congress
(October 19, 1765)

The main points of contention among the colonists in America were clearly expressed by the Stamp Act Congress in the 14 resolutions they passed. Two of the most important were:

That His Majesty's liege subjects in these colonies, are entitled to all the inherent rights *and liberties of his natural born subjects within the kingdom of Great-Britain.*

That it is inseparably essential to the freedom of a people, and the undoubted right of Englishmen, that no taxes be imposed on them, but with their own consent, given personally, or by their representatives.

THE TOWNSHEND DUTIES
1767

In the debate over the Stamp Act, many colonial leaders, including Benjamin Franklin, made the distinction between an internal tax, that was meant to directly tax people within the colony, and an external tax. An external tax was one put on transactions and events that took place between parts of the British Empire. Duties on trade were considered external taxes. With this argument in mind, Parliament passed a series of duties on goods that were imported into the colonies from other parts of the British Empire. Duties were placed on glass, paper, lead, painter's colors, and tea. The money from these duties was to be used to pay the salaries of Crown officials in the colonies. Before this, officials had depended on colonial assemblies to raise money to pay them.

In New Hampshire, the reaction to the Townshend Duties was much less than the furor caused by the Stamp Act. However, in both Boston and New York, the Townshend Duties led to violence. In New York, on January 18, 1770, after a long period of confrontations between British soldiers and protestors, a riot broke out and many on both sides were injured. In Boston, a few months later, on March 5, 1770, the demonstrators were not as lucky. This time the British soldiers fired into the crowd, killing five colonists and seriously wounding six others.

Once again, Parliament realized that their attempt to tax the colonies had failed. Most of the Townshend Duties were repealed in April 1770. The duty on tea was kept mainly as a symbolic gesture by Parliament to show that they were in control. The repeal of the rest of the Townshend Duties caused the situation in the colonies to quiet down. At this point, very few people in the colonies wanted independence from Britain. What they wanted was more self-rule and the same rights as people living in Britain. But the thought of an armed uprising against the king was far from the thoughts of most people. It was Parliament's attempt to once again tax the colonies that ultimately led to war.

On May 10, 1773, Parliament passed the Tea Act in an attempt to help bail out the British East India Company, which was on the verge of going bankrupt. The Tea Act was intended to stop the importation of non-British tea into the colonies. The tax on tea was actually reduced from that remaining under the Townshend Duties, but it

New Hampshire Loyalists

One reason that protests in New Hampshire were not as forceful as in some other colonies was the fact that Portsmouth was a center of Loyalist feelings. Many have suggested that by the time of the Revolutionary War, the 2.5 million people in the colonies were divided into three relatively equal groups. One third of the people were opposed to continued British rule and these people were referred to as Whigs. Another third remained loyal to the king and Britain and were called Loyalists or Tories. The final third were neutral. The wealthy merchants of New Hampshire, led by Governor Wentworth, were dependent on contracts with the government in London for their lucrative trade in naval timber products. They tried to keep New Hampshire loyal to the Crown.

An inventor of innovative fireplaces and other household devices using heat, Benjamin Thompson, Count Rumford, was a well-known Loyalist, who moved to London in 1776. *(Collections of the State of New Hampshire Division of Historical Resources)*

gave the East India Company a monopoly that was against the ideas of free enterprise that had developed in the colonies. Once again, the powers in London had misread how the colonies would react.

On December 16, 1773, after the first load of tea under the new Tea Act arrived in Boston, a group of about 60 members of the Sons of Liberty disguised as Native Americans, with a large crowd looking on, boarded the three tea ships and threw 340 chests of tea into the harbor. This event is known as the Boston Tea Party. Similar "tea parties" were later held in Charleston, South Carolina; New York; New Jersey; and Maryland.

To protest the passage of the Tea Act, some male colonists, disguised as American Indians, boarded three ships in Boston Harbor on December 16, 1773, and dumped hundreds of cases of tea into the harbor. The event became known as the Boston Tea Party. *(Library of Congress)*

In New Hampshire, a group that wanted to follow Boston's lead was convinced by Governor Wentworth at a town meeting that their boycott of British tea would be enough. A crowd of people protesting the Tea Act did attack the tea agent's house, throwing rocks through the windows. It would take another act of Parliament to finally make the people of New Hampshire and elsewhere realize that the situation was getting serious and that drastic actions might be needed.

THE COERCIVE ACTS
1774

Parliament and the other leaders in London were extremely upset by the Boston Tea Party and felt it was time to teach the colonies a lesson. To do this, they passed a series of laws that were intended to punish the people of Boston and regain control of all the colonies. In Parliament, the bills were called the Coercive Acts. In the colonies, they were referred to as the Intolerable Acts. The first act was called the Boston Port Bill, and it closed the port of Boston until the people of Boston paid for the £10,000 worth of tea that had been dumped in the harbor. The second act was called the

Massachusetts Government Act, and it changed the Massachusetts charter. The changes took power from the people of Massachusetts and gave it to Crown officials.

There were also acts that were intended to make it easier to convict people of violations against imperial regulations, and one provided religious toleration for the Catholics in Canada, as well as extending the borders of Canada. This took away lands to the west that were claimed by a number of colonies. The final act was one that had a large impact in New Hampshire. The Quartering Act, passed on May 3, 1765, was intended to charge the colonies for the housing and maintenance of British troops that were being sent to the colonies to enforce the other Intolerable Acts.

Instead of getting the people of the colonies to give in to the Crown, the Intolerable Acts had the opposite effect. Throughout the colonies, people saw what was being done to Boston and Massachusetts and realized that their own colonial governments and other institutions could be changed at the whim of Parliament. People throughout the colonies rallied to supply food and other essential goods to Boston by shipping them to other ports nearby and then taking them overland to Boston. Colonial leaders were so concerned about the situation that a call went out to the Committees of Correspondence for a Continental Congress to present a united response to Parliament and its Intolerable Acts.

Governor Wentworth's Carpenters

Up until the passing of the Intolerable Acts, there had been an uneasy peace between the people of New Hampshire and their Loyalist governor. John Wentworth had replaced his uncle Benning Wentworth as governor in 1767. He had walked a narrow line between carrying out his royal duties and providing reasonable leadership for the people of New Hampshire. It was his leadership that had tempered the protest movement in New Hampshire. However, in 1774, when troops were sent to Boston under the Quartering Act, the British could not find anyone in Boston willing to build barracks for the troops. General Thomas Gage turned to the governor of New Hampshire for help. Wentworth showed his true colors as a Loyalist when he sent carpenters from New Hampshire to build barracks for the British troops in Boston, which upset many in New Hampshire.

THE FIRST CONTINENTAL CONGRESS
1774

In New Hampshire, as in many other colonies, the royal government wanted nothing to do with a Continental Congress. Governor Wentworth disbanded the assembly in an effort to prevent New Hampshire from participating in the Continental Congress. Therefore, a separate provincial congress was held in July 1774. They met in Exeter and chose John Sullivan and Nathaniel Folsom to represent New Hampshire at the Continental Congress. On September 5, 1774, 56 delegates from the thirteen colonies arrived in Philadelphia, Pennsylvania, to hold the First Continental Congress. A few of the more radical delegates wanted to move toward independence, but the vast majority were still looking for a way to reconcile with Parliament and the Crown.

After almost two months of debate, a series of resolutions were drafted and sent to the king. The delegates also agreed to support a series of nonviolent actions that primarily involved embargoes against trading with Great Britain. They also agreed to return the following year to evaluate the progress they had made in solving their problems with London.

THE CAPTURE OF FORT WILLIAM AND MARY
December 14, 1774

Nearly two months after the Continental Congress adjourned, Paul Revere, the Boston silversmith and messenger for the Boston Committee of Correspondence, rode into Portsmouth. His message was

The Resolutions of the First Continental Congress

After listing numerous complaints with the attempts by Parliament to impose its will on the American colonies, the document sent to the king by the First Continental Congress made it clear that the Americans were planning boycott, not revolution.

Resolved, unanimously, That from and after the first day of December next, there be no importation into British America, from Great Britain or Ireland of any goods, wares or merchandize whatsoever, or from any other place of any such goods, wares or merchandize.

The night of April 18, 1775, Paul Revere completed his midnight ride, during which he warned colonists that the British were heading inland from Boston. *(National Archives/DOD, War & Conflict, #8)*

the same as it would be in April 1775 when he would make his famous ride to Lexington and Concord, "the British are coming." Revere wanted the more radical elements in New Hampshire to be warned that the British in Boston were sending a much larger force to man Fort William and Mary. The fort had been built during King William's War to defend Portsmouth Harbor from attack by the French. The fort was garrisoned by one officer and five soldiers.

On December 14, 1774, roughly 400 New Hampshire Whigs led by John Sullivan and John Langdon gathered in Portsmouth and marched on the fort. The soldiers fired their small cannon in an attempt to scare off the mob. Undeterred, the Patriots rushed the fort from all sides and quickly captured the six men. The fort was stripped of its cannons and guns. Even more valuable were the

Depicted in this undated drawing, Fort William and Mary is located on New Castle Island in Portsmouth Harbor. *(New Hampshire Historical Society)*

100 barrels of gunpowder. The military supplies were hidden near Sullivan's home in Durham. Governor Wentworth ordered that all involved in the attack on the fort be arrested, but he had no soldiers to do it. It is believed that the powder ended up supplying the Patriot forces at the Battle of Bunker Hill in Charlestown, Massachusetts, where a contingent of New Hampshire militiamen fought.

Governor Wentworth and his family soon realized that the situation was now beyond their control. They fled to safety in Halifax, Nova Scotia, in June 1775. John Wentworth served the Crown in Canada, where he died in 1820. Despite his many years in Canada, Governor Wentworth reportedly considered New Hampshire his "native land" until the end of his life.

9

The War for Independence

LEXINGTON, CONCORD, AND BUNKER HILL
1775

As tensions rose between the British soldiers stationed in Boston and the Patriot leaders of Massachusetts, militia groups throughout the colonies were organized and began to drill in anticipation of war. On April 18, 1775, British troops marched out of Boston and headed for Lexington and Concord in hopes of catching some of the Patriot leaders who had already left the area. The next morning, April 19, 1775, when the British reached Lexington Green, they were met by a small force of local militia. When ordered to lay down their weapons by the much larger British force, the Patriots broke ranks and tried to escape. The British soldiers opened fire and killed eight colonists and wounded 10 others.

When word spread of the shooting in Lexington, militias from all over the area were mobilized. By the time the British reached Concord, they were met by a much larger colonial force. A pitched battle was fought at the North Bridge in Concord, and then it was the British soldiers' turn to try and escape. As they retreated to Boston, they were harassed by militia sharpshooters who fired at them from the cover of the woods or the protection of stone walls. The British soldiers suffered 300 dead or wounded, while the Americans lost about 100 fighters. The American Revolution was now a reality.

Second in command of Rogers's Rangers during the French and Indian War, John Stark also fought in the Battles of Bunker Hill and Bennington during the Revolutionary War. *(National Archives, Still Picture Records, NWDNS-148-GW-137)*

By April 20, 1775, the news of the Battle of Lexington and Concord had spread to New Hampshire and throughout New England. It was soon news in all the colonies. The hopes of reconciliation with the Crown and Parliament had gone up in the clouds of smoke issued from the guns of war. Militia units headed for Boston with hopes of driving the British into the harbor. Thirty-five men from Epsom, New Hampshire, made the 75-mile march to Cambridge, Massachusetts, in 24 hours. Henry Dearborn led 100 militia from Epping 60 miles south in 12 hours. More came from every town in New Hampshire, and by the end of April, there were more than 2,000 Patriots from New Hampshire in Massachusetts ready to fight the British for control of Boston. John Stark, who had been second in command of Rogers's Rangers during the French and Indian War, was put in charge of the New Hampshire contingent. Soon, there were more than 16,000 colonial soldiers surrounding Boston.

For the next two months, there were no major conflicts between the colonial militias that had gathered around Boston and the British forces that were trapped there. The militia leaders knew they needed to command the high ground around Boston and its harbor if they were going to drive out the British. Plans were made to fortify Dorchester Heights to the south of the city and Breed's and Bunker Hills, which overlook the harbor from Charlestown to the north. During the night of June 16, 1775, about 1,000 colonial militia, many of them from New Hampshire, went to the top of Breed's and Bunker Hills. It was decided that they would dig in on Breed's Hill, which was not quite as tall as Bunker Hill but was closer to the harbor.

When the British soldiers in Boston woke up on June 17, 1775, they were greeted with the sight of the colonial force looking

John Stark
(1728–1822)

John Stark was born in Londonderry, New Hampshire, and later moved with his family to Derryfield, which is now part of Manchester, New Hampshire. As Robert Rogers's second in command, he had been one of the heroes of the French and Indian War. In spring 1752, he was checking his traps with his brother William, Amos Eastman, and another friend. The four were surprised by a raiding party from the Christian Indian town of St. Francis in Canada.

William Stark was able to escape. John Stark and Amos Eastman were captured and the other friend was killed.

The two captives were marched north to St. Francis, where they were forced to "run the gauntlet." This was a way Native Americans tortured their prisoners. Men and women from the village would form in two lines while holding sticks and clubs. A prisoner would be forced to run down between the lines, and he or she would be

(continues)

One way American Indians tortured prisoners was to have them "run the gauntlet." In this engraving, published in an 1839 book, a young boy named Frederick Schermerhorn begins the perilous journey between the waiting rows, similar to the situation John Stark faced as a prisoner. *(Library of Congress, Prints and Photographs Division [LC-USZ62-71109])*

(continued)

hit repeatedly. Eastman went first and received a serious beating. Not wanting to suffer the fate of his friend, Stark grabbed a club from one of the warriors at the beginning of the line and fought back.

The people of St. Francis were so impressed by this act of bravery that they nicknamed him "young chief." Stark was adopted into the community and learned the Abenaki language and ways. He was such a valued prisoner that when officials from Massachusetts came to ransom them, they were charged $63 for Eastman but had to pay $103 for Stark.

During the Revolutionary War, John Stark rose to the rank of general, and he and his New Hampshire soldiers were involved in many battles. The two most important to the war effort were the Battle of Bunker Hill and the Battle of Bennington. Stark lived to be 93 years old.

"Whites of Their Eyes"

"Don't one of you fire until you see the whites of their eyes," Colonel William Prescott is reported to have said to his men as the British troops marched up Breed's Hill.

down their rifles at them. The British response was immediate. Warships were brought in to bombard Breed's Hill. Then a force of 2,200 redcoats, as the British soldiers were called, was sent to show the colonials what it was like to face an assault by troops from the greatest army in the world at the time.

General Gage, the British commander, blundered when he instructed General Howe to lead his forces in a direct frontal assault. The British learned a very hard lesson on the slopes of Breed's Hill. Instead of panicking in the face of 2,200 British soldiers marching up the hill in formation, Colonel William Prescott had his troops hold their fire until the British were almost to them. When the order to fire was given, the colonial marksmen mowed down the British soldiers and sent them retreating down the hill.

Once out of range, the British reset their formations and marched into the colonial sights again. The results were the same: The British suffered even more casualties and were sent back down again. On the third assault, the British finally captured Breed's Hill because the colonials had run out of gunpowder, but British losses were so heavy, they were unable to pursue the American fighters. Records show that 226 British soldiers died and 828 were wounded in capturing Breed's Hill. On the colonial side, 140 were killed and 271 were wounded.

The Battle of Bunker Hill on June 17, 1775, helped the colonists realize they might have a chance at becoming independent from the British. *(Library of Congress)*

The American Revolution was just starting, and the Battle of Bunker Hill, as it is called, was not a significant victory in terms of territory won and lost. However, in the psychological battle between the mighty British army and the untrained and undisciplined American forces, the impact of the battle on the slopes of Breed's Hill was immense. From this battle forward, the British proceeded with much greater respect for their adversaries and with a sense of caution. Although the colonials lost the hill, they gained a huge boost of confidence. They may not have had fancy red uniforms, but the minutemen of New Hampshire, Massachusetts, and other colonies that held in the face of the attacks on Breed's Hill had proved they were a match for the British regulars.

General Gage had now commanded two attacks against the colonial forces. At both Lexington and Concord, and at Breed's Hill, his forces had been shown up by the colonials. When word of the casualties sustained at Breed's Hill reached London, Gage was recalled. General William Howe took over as commander of the British forces in North America. Some have argued that it was

Excerpt from the New Hampshire Constitution
(1776)

In the second paragraph of New Hampshire's 1776 constitution, the legislators made their position clear but still left the door open for reconciliation with Britain.

The sudden and abrupt departure of his Excellency John Wentworth, Esq., our late Governor, and several of the Council, leaving us destitute of legislation, and no executive courts being open to punish criminal offenders; whereby the lives and properties of the honest people of this colony are liable to the machinations and evil designs of wicked men, Therefore, *for the preservation of peace and good order, and for the security of the lives and properties of the inhabitants of this colony, we conceive ourselves reduced to the necessity of establishing A FORM OF GOVERNMENT to continue during the present unhappy and unnatural contest with Great Britain; PROTESTING and DECLARING that we neaver sought to throw off our dependence upon Great Britain, but felt ourselves happy under her protection, while we could enjoy our constitutional rights and privileges. And that we shall rejoice if such a reconciliation between us and our parent State can be effected as shall be approved by the CONTINENTAL CONGRESS, in whose prudence and wisdom we confide.*

Howe's cautious attitude, after leading the attack on Breed's Hill, that may have been the ultimate key to an American victory in the War for Independence.

NEW HAMPSHIRE DECLARES INDEPENDENCE

When the call went out for the Second Continental Congress, New Hampshire's provincial assembly reconvened. They again selected John Sullivan to represent them in Philadelphia. They also selected John Langdon as a delegate. Langdon and Sullivan had led the attack on Fort William and Mary and were active Whig leaders.

The provincial assembly continued to expand its role as the governing body of New Hampshire. The colonial government had collapsed with the departure of Governor Wentworth. By December 1775, a new provincial assembly had been elected, and they began to debate a constitution. On January 5, 1776, the provincial assembly passed a new constitution for New Hampshire. They were the first state to make it clear that they intended to take charge of their own government by creating a new constitution for the state.

The delegates to the Continental Congress in Philadelphia debated what action they should take and organized the fight to get the British out of Boston. George Washington was put in charge of the Continental army and John Sullivan of New Hampshire became one of his generals. By early summer, it seemed likely that the colonies would declare their independence from Great Britain. New Hampshire made it clear that it was ready for

The First Paragraph of the Declaration of Independence

Thomas Jefferson of Virginia is given credit as being the primary author of the Declaration of Independence. He began it with the following paragraph:

When in the Course of human events, it becomes necessary for one people to dissolve the political bands which have connected them with another, and to assume among the Powers of the earth, the separate and equal station to which the Laws of Nature and of Nature's God entitle them, a decent respect to the opinions of mankind requires that they should declare the causes which impel them to the separation.

The Second Continental Congress selected a committee of five members to draft the Declaration of Independence. From left to right are Benjamin Franklin, Thomas Jefferson, Robert Livingston, John Adams, and Roger Sherman. *(Library of Congress)*

Matthew Thornton represented New Hampshire at the Second Continental Congress and signed the Declaration of Independence on the colony's behalf. *(Collections of the State of New Hampshire Division of Historical Resources)*

independence by issuing their own Declaration of Independence on June 15, 1776.

By this time, Sullivan and Langdon had left Philadelphia to participate directly in the war. New Hampshire replaced them with three other delegates. Josiah Bartlett, Matthew Thornton, and William Whipple were the ones who signed the Declaration of Independence that was passed by the Continental Congress on July 4, 1776.

Independence was easier to declare than it was to achieve. The War of Independence would go on until British general Lord Cornwallis surrendered at Yorktown, Virginia, on October 19, 1781. In the early years of the war, it looked like independence might not be achieved. Although no battles were fought in New Hampshire, soldiers from the state fought throughout the war in all parts of the struggle. General John Stark from New Hampshire led soldiers from New Hampshire, Massachusetts, and Vermont to a critical victory.

American forces capture strategic positions on October 14, 1781, at the Battle of Yorktown. Five days later, this particular battle and the Revolutionary War would end with Britain's surrender. *(National Archives, Still Picture Records, NWDNS-148-GW-565)*

THE BATTLE OF BENNINGTON
August 16, 1777

British General John Burgoyne left Canada with a large army of British regulars and Hessian mercenaries. His plan was to capture Albany, New York, and divide New England from the states to the south. Burgoyne's force moved easily down Lake Champlain and captured Fort Ticonderoga. However, the American forces deployed a number of tactics meant to delay Burgoyne's attempt to march on Albany. The tactics worked and Burgoyne began to run short of supplies.

Burgoyne sent out a force of between 500 and 700 Hessians to scour the countryside for supplies. Instead, when they got close to Bennington, Vermont, they found General John Stark leading a force of 1,400 militia from Massachusetts and New Hampshire. They were joined by Ethan Allen and the Green Mountain Boys. In the battle that took place, the Americans captured the Hessian force and then captured another force that had been sent out to help the Hessians.

Hessians

To ensure they had sufficient troops to fight the American rebels, the British hired German mercenaries called Hessians. These were professional soldiers who were used in a variety of ways by the British.

Led by General John Stark, the colonial forces experienced a momentous victory at the Battle of Bennington on August 16, 1777. *(National Archives, Still Picture Records, NWDNS-111-SC-96740)*

Vermont and the Green Mountain Boys

At the time of the Revolution, there was an area of conflicting claims between New York and New Hampshire. The area was thinly populated. In 1764, the king's Privy Council ruled that the area that would eventually become Vermont was part of New York. Many people in the area had received their land claims from New Hampshire. The people of Vermont, under the leadership of Ethan Allen, his two brothers Ira and Levi, and his cousin Seth Warner, organized a militia known as the Green Mountain Boys to prevent New York officials from taking over their land.

When fighting broke out against the British, Ethan Allen and the Green Mountain boys fought as Patriots to drive the British out of Ticonderoga and Crown Point. On January 15, 1777, the people of Vermont declared their independence from both New Hampshire and New York. They created an independent republic. Vermont remained independent until it was admitted to the Union as the 14th state on March 4, 1791.

Instead of getting needed supplies, Burgoyne lost a large part of his army. When the British reached Saratoga, New York, they found General Horatio Gates and 10,000 American soldiers waiting for them. They would get no further. After losing two separate battles at Saratoga, Burgoyne had no choice but to surrender on

Appointed commander in chief of the British forces in Canada in spring 1777, General John Burgoyne surrendered at Saratoga on October 17, 1777, a significant American victory in the Revolutionary War. (*National Archives*)

October 17, 1777. Many consider this American victory at Saratoga the turning point in the war. Without Stark's victory at Bennington, the outcome at Saratoga, and the entire war, might have been different.

THE WAR AT SEA

On October 13, 1775, the Continental Congress authorized the creation of a Continental navy. However, the cost of building ships and maintaining a navy was more than the Continental Congress was able to afford. The small navy that resulted was used more to harass British merchants than to fight the Royal Navy. During the Revolutionary War, three ships were built for the Continental navy in Portsmouth, New Hampshire. They were the 72-gun *Raleigh* in 1776, the 18-gun *Ranger* in 1777, and the 74-gun *America* in 1782. The Continental navy was disbanded at the end of the war, and the *America* was presented to the king of France for his help during the Revolutionary War.

Three ships were built in Portsmouth, New Hampshire, for the Continental navy. Although the Continental navy was dissolved after the war, the United States established a permanent navy in 1798. This engraving shows the U.S. Navy Yard in Portsmouth. *(New Hampshire Historical Society)*

The *Ranger* was commanded by John Paul Jones and was out-fitted with a crew made up predominantly of New Hampshire sailors and officers. In 1777, Jones and his crew sailed the *Ranger* to France and then attacked British shipping in the English Channel and elsewhere along the coast of Great Britain. Two years later,

John Paul Jones leads the capture of the *Serapis.* *(National Archives)*

John Paul Jones
(1747–1792)

Born John Paul in Scotland in 1747, John Paul Jones first came to America at the age of 12 as a cabin boy on a merchant ship. He quickly rose through the ranks and became the first mate on a ship involved in the slave trade while still in his teens. He seems to have been a very harsh captain. In 1770, he flogged (whipped) one of his crewmen, who later died. He was acquitted by the courts but soon found himself in trouble again.

In 1773, he was imprisoned in Tobago, a British island in the Caribbean, when he shot and killed a member of his crew who was allegedly leading a mutiny. Rather than wait in prison for his trial, he escaped and returned to the colonies. The British authorities considered him a pirate and fugitive. It was at this time that he added *Jones* to his name to avoid capture by British authorities.

After the Revolutionary War ended, he was the only naval officer to be awarded a gold medal by the Congress. When the navy was disbanded, Jones went to Russia and served in the navy of Catherine the Great. He later retired to Paris, where he died in 1792.

John Paul Jones, a hero of the Revolutionary War, was awarded a gold medal by Congress. *(National Archives)*

on September 23, 1779, off the British coast, while commanding a converted merchant ship that had been renamed the *Bonhomme Richard*, Jones defeated the British warship *Serapis*. This battle is one of the most famous in naval history, and it is where Jones is reported to have said, when asked if he was ready to surrender, "I have not yet begun to fight!"

Despite the limited resources of the Continental navy, the Patriots were able to cause serious damage to the shipping of the British. During the Revolution, as many as 800 private ships sailed with Letters of Marque and Reprisal issued by both the Continental Congress and the individual states. A ship carrying one of these letters was called a privateer and was authorized to attack any and all enemy ships.

It has been estimated that the damage done to British shipping would have a value today of more than $300 million. More than 100 of these privateers sailed out of Portsmouth, New Hampshire. As many as 3,000 New Hampshire men sailed in either the Continental navy or as privateers during the Revolutionary War.

During the war years, New Hampshire had grown and prospered. When peace finally came with the Treaty of Paris in 1783, the 13 colonies had won their independence from Great Britain and now looked forward to becoming a nation.

10

Becoming One State and a Part of the Nation

The relative prosperity of the war years was followed by a time of both economic and political uncertainty in New Hampshire and throughout the 13 united states. The Continental Congress and most of the states had borrowed heavily to finance the war effort. Paper money issued by both the states and the Congress had lost much of its value. After the war, it took £40 of Continental currency to buy £1 worth of goods. Many of the soldiers who had fought in the war were never paid or paid with nearly worthless paper money. Individual debt became a serious

The Continental Congress issued paper money during and after the Revolutionary War that became worthless. *(From Benson Lossing,* The Pictorial Field-Book of the Revolution, *1851–1852)*

problem, especially since the vast majority of people in the colonies were farmers.

During the war, farm goods had brought high prices as large amounts of food were needed to support the army. When all the soldiers returned home after the war, farm production increased, but the demand for surplus farm produce dropped off. In western

A Revolutionary War general, delegate to the first Continental Congress, and member of the Second Continental Congress, among other honors, John Sullivan became governor of New Hampshire in 1786. *(Library of Congress, Prints and Photographs Division [LC-USZ62-39567])*

Massachusetts, an armed rebellion led by Daniel Shays threatened the stability of the state and required the militia to be called in.

In New Hampshire, a large and angry mob marched on the legislature in Exeter on September 20, 1786. General John Sullivan was the president of the legislature at the time, and he did not wait for trouble to start. He immediately called out the militia. By the morning of September 21, more than 2,000 militiamen surrounded Exeter. In the face of such overwhelming force, the protestors backed down. The immediate crisis was avoided without a shot being fired, but the bigger problem still needed to be solved.

THE ARTICLES OF CONFEDERATION

The Second Continental Congress had proposed the Articles of Confederation in 1777. They were finally adopted by the states in 1781. Under the articles, there was a loose confederation of the states and a very weak federal authority. Those who had proposed the articles did not want a strong central government. They wanted the bulk of the power to remain with the states. The experience of the tyrannical abuses of the British government in dealing with the colonies made many leery of giving much if any power to a central government.

During the war, the Continental Congress had acted on behalf of the country without any real official status. The Articles of Confederation were designed to formalize the union of the 13 separate states. On paper, the articles seemed like a good compromise between those who wanted a stronger federal government and those who did not.

However, when implemented, there were numerous problems. The biggest obstacle was that the federal government lacked any way to raise revenue other than asking the states for money. The federal government also had no way to enforce its laws. In addition, the articles set up a very difficult decision-making process. Each state, no matter its size, was given one vote. Often delegations could not come to a consensus on an issue and would not be able to cast a vote. This created another problem. The articles required all 13 states to agree before any action could be taken by the federal government.

The Articles of Confederation, shown here, were written by a committee of the Continental Congress and intended as a constitution for the colonies. *(National Archives, National Archives Building, NWCTB-360-MISC-ROLL10F81)*

Under the Articles of Confederation, at times the 13 states functioned completely independently of each other. Sometimes this put the states in opposition to each other in terms of trade and issues of boundaries. Shays's Rebellion, the protests at Exeter, and similar events in other colonies made it apparent to many that a stronger central government was needed. Those in favor of a stronger central government were known as Federalists. It was these people who lobbied for a Constitutional Convention to change the government by amending or replacing the Articles of Confederation.

THE CONSTITUTIONAL CONVENTION, 1787

New Hampshire had gone to work before the Revolution was even over and begun the process of creating a new constitution for the state. A constitution drawn up in 1779 was rejected by the voters of the state, and another state constitutional convention was held in Concord in 1781. This constitution was modeled in part on the one that Massachusetts had adopted. However, one of the problems faced by the framers of the New Hampshire constitution was the regionalism in the state. Communication followed the river valleys, which made it hard for the people along the Connecticut and Merrimack Rivers to communicate with one another and with the communities along the seacoast.

Another problem was making sure that all the people of the state had an equal voice in the legislature. To do this, the new constitution made sure that every citizen had equal representation. This created a very large House of Representatives. Today, the New Hampshire legislature is the largest in the country. The constitution created in 1783 was passed by the voters of the state and went into effect in 1784.

Active in New Hampshire's early political life, John Langdon not only represented the state at the Constitutional Convention, he also served as president of the colony for two years and governor of the state for eight years. *(Collections of the State of New Hampshire Division of Historical Resources)*

Preamble to the U.S. Constitution

We the People of the United States, in Order to form a more perfect Union, establish Justice, insure domestic Tranquility, provide for the common defence, promote the general Welfare, and secure the Blessings of Liberty to ourselves and our Posterity, do ordain and establish this Constitution for the United States of America.

Having created a new constitution for the state, many in New Hampshire saw the need for a new constitution for the federal government. New Hampshire sent John Langdon and Nicholas Gilman to the Constitutional Convention in Philadelphia, which began in May 1787. The first action taken by the delegates to the convention was to decide that the Articles of Confederation were too flawed and an entirely new constitution was needed. There were many issues that had to be dealt with by the delegates, and one of the most important was about representation.

The small states, like New Hampshire, wanted each state to have equal representation. The plan they put forward was called the New Jersey Plan because it had been written by the delegates from that state. The Virginia Plan was put forward by the delegates of the largest state and it called for representation based on population. It looked liked the delegates had hit an impasse.

The delegates from Connecticut came up with what is known as the "Great Compromise," which called for two legislative bodies: a senate that is based on equal representation for every state, and a House of Representatives that is based on population. This compromise was accepted by all the delegations and is the way the federal and most state legislatures are organized today. Once they had agreed on the Constitution, the delegates decided it would require the approval of nine of the 13 states to make it law.

The Constitution was passed by the convention on September 17, 1787, and was sent out to the states for ratification. On December 7, 1787, Delaware was the first state to ratify the new Constitution. By the time the New Hampshire ratifying convention met in June 1788, eight states had ratified the Constitution. Only one more was needed to make it law.

When the delegates gathered in Concord, there was strong support for rejecting the new constitution. Many felt that it gave the federal government too much power. General John Sullivan, now the governor of the state, was chairman of the convention, and he oversaw the debate. Josiah Bartlett, who had signed the Declaration of Independence, worked for ratification, as did many other Patriot leaders. One of the speeches that is credited with swaying the delegates was made by Colonel Ebenezer Webster, the father of Daniel Webster.

On June 21, 1788, the delegates in Concord voted 57 to 47 in favor of the new Constitution. New Hampshire was the ninth state to ratify the Constitution, and it became the governing document of the United States and remains so today.

Signer of the Declaration of Independence on behalf of New Hampshire, Josiah Bartlett governed New Hampshire from 1791 to 1792. *(Collections of the State of New Hampshire Division of Historical Resources)*

Ebenezer Webster's Speech to the New Hampshire Ratifying Convention

I have listened to the arguments for and against the Constitution. I am convinced such a government as that constitution will establish, if adopted—a government acting directly on the people of the States—is necessary for the common defense and general welfare. It is the only government which will enable us to pay off the national debt—the debt we owe for the Revolution, and which we are bound in honor fully and fairly to discharge. Besides, I have followed the lead of Washington through seven years of war, and I have never been misled. His name is subscribed to this constitution. He will not mislead us now. I shall vote for its adoption.

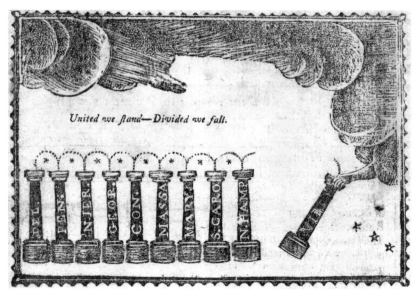

Published in the *New Hampshire Gazette* on June 26, 1788, this illustration includes nine upright pillars, representing the first nine colonies to ratify the Constitution. At the time of ratification, each colony became a state, and as the Constitutional Convention delegates had agreed, the ratification of it by nine states made the Constitution law. *(New Hampshire Historical Society)*

When word spread that the Constitution had been ratified, the people of the state turned out for a huge celebration in Portsmouth on June 26, 1788. The people of New Hampshire were proud to be the ones who put the Constitution into place. The residents of New Hampshire still retain the individualism and independence that helped them overcome great odds to become one of our original 13 states.

New Hampshire
Time Line

11,000–9,000 B.C.

★ The first evidence of Native Americans in New Hampshire is during the Paleo-Indian period.

1602

★ Captain Bartholomew Gosnold lands on New Hampshire coast, the first documented European landing.

1603

★ Martin Pring, an English captain, explores the Piscataqua River, near present-day Portsmouth.

1605

★ Samuel de Champlain explores the New Hampshire coast and the Isles of Shoals.

1614

★ John Smith sails along the New England coast.

1622

★ John Mason and Fernando Gorges are given a grant to much of the land that is now Maine and New Hampshire. Mason spends

£22,000 to clear land and have houses built. Mason dies in 1635 without coming to America.

1623

★ Captain John Mason under his land grant sends David Thomson from Scotland, and Edward and Thomas Hilton, fish merchants from London, with other settlers to establish a fishing colony at the mouth of the Piscataqua, the first permanent settlement in New Hampshire. The group under Thomson settles near the mouth of the Piscataqua River. They call the settlement "Little Harbor" or "Pannaway" (present-day Rye). The other group under the Hiltons set up fishing operations eight miles north in an area they call Northam, now Dover.

1645

★ The first recorded slave arrives in Portsmouth.

1670

★ By 1670, relations between the Europeans and the Native Americans begin to deteriorate as the European-settler population grows. The Native American population goes from tens of thousands at first contact to 1,200 by the end of the 17th century.

1679

★ New Hampshire is established as a British royal province separate from Massachusetts, under President John Cutt.

1685

★ New Hampshire becomes part of the Dominion of New England.

1689

★ **June 27:** The Pennacook attack Dover, killing 24. The attack is precipitated by Richard Waldron.

1698

★ New Hampshire goes under Massachusetts's governor Joseph Dudley's jurisdiction.

1717

★ John Wentworth becomes lieutenant governor of New Hampshire.

1719

★ Due to unrest in Britain, Scots living in Londonderry, Ireland, come to New Hampshire to form their own colony, which they name Londonderry.

1740

★ New Hampshire's eastern and southern borders are established by a royal commission.

1741

★ New Hampshire is established as a separate colony under Governor Benning Wentworth, who stayed in office from 1741–66.

1745

★ Four hundred fifty New Hampshire troops under Colonel Samuel Moore joined other colonies and British at the siege of Louisbourg, Cape Breton, where they defeat the French.

1763

★ The Treaty of Paris is signed, marking the victory of England over France.

1770

★ After Benning Wentworth's death, his nephew, who later became Sir John Wentworth, becomes governor (the last royal governor). Wentworth buys a 36-mile tract on Lake Winnepesaukee, where he has an estate he calls Kingwood, which later becomes Wolfeborough. John Wentworth also builds roads, including one from Portsmouth to Kingswood, and organizes a militia, including Major Benjamin Thompson of Concord, later called Count Rumford.

★ Dartmouth College is chartered, with help from Benning Wentworth. It is initially for Native Americans. It is the first college in New Hampshire.

1774

★ **May:** The Committee of Correspondence in Portsmouth writes to the committee in Boston, promising their support.

★ **June 8:** Governor Wentworth dissolves the assembly (which he has done before).

★ **July 4:** Twenty-seven chests of tea are dumped into Portsmouth harbor. A town meeting is called, and a ship containing the remaining tea is guarded and then sails for Halifax.

★ **July 6:** Governor Wentworth has a sheriff disperse the Committee of Correspondence, which is meeting to choose delegates for an American congress. The committee does choose delegates, but they do it privately.

★ **December 13:** Paul Revere rides to New Hampshire to alert Samuel Cutts of the Portsmouth Committee that the British are coming to Portsmouth to reinforce the fort there and to remove the gunpowder and the guns that are being stored. The gunpowder and guns are later used by the Patriots at the Battle of Bunker Hill. Cutts holds a committee meeting, which decides to attack the fort.

★ **December 14:** Fort William and Mary is attacked at midnight by roughly 400 men from Portsmouth, Rye, and Newcastle who march through Portsmouth. They are fired upon by the five British soldiers who are under the command of Captain Cochran at the fort. The Patriots storm the fort and remove 100 barrels of gunpowder. They then send the gunpowder up the Piscataqua River to Durham.

★ **December 15:** A second attack is made on Fort William and Mary by men from Durham under John Sullivan. They remove the lighter cannons and all the guns from the fort.

★ **December 16:** The Patriots under Captain Nathaniel Folsom of Exeter arrive in Portsmouth and guard the fort all day. They then send the arms up to Durham by water.

★ Although no actual battles are fought in New Hampshire during the Revolution, they keep three regiments in the Continental Line and fight at Bunker Hill, Trenton, Bennington, Saratoga, Monmouth, and Yorktown.

1775

★ **June:** Governor John Wentworth and his family flee.

★ **June 17:** The Battle of Bunker Hill is fought. John Stark and New Hampshire troops fight at Bunker Hill, forming the majority of troops who fight there.

★ **December:** John Paul Jones, originally from Scotland, more recently of New Hampshire, is commissioned.

1776

★ **January:** A provisional government is established after Governor Wentworth flees to Nova Scotia in response to the Patriots.

★ **January 5:** A state constitution is written at a meeting in Exeter, the first colony to do so.

★ **July:** The Declaration of Independence is signed in Philadelphia by New Hampshire's Josiah Bartlett, Matthew Thornton, and William Whipple.

1777

★ **August 16:** New Hampshire troops under John Stark fight at the Battle of Bennington.

1778

★ A Constitutional Convention is called.

1782

★ The first elected representatives meet at the General Court in Concord.

1784

★ A second state constitution is written (it is still used, with amendments).

1788

★ New Hampshire becomes the ninth state.

New Hampshire Historical Sites

CHARLESTOWN

Fort at No. 4   A living-history museum and replica of the original fort built in 1743 where 18th-century crafts and skills are demonstrated.

> *Address:* Springfield Road, Route 11, Charlestown, NH 03603
> *Phone:* 888-367-8824
> *Web Site:* www.fortat4.com

CONCORD

Museum of New Hampshire History   The Museum of New Hampshire History has exhibits on New Hampshire history as well as a Hands-on-History Family Center.

> *Address:* The Hamel Center, 6 Eagle Center, Concord, NH 03301
> *Phone:* 603-228-6688
> *Web Site:* www.nhhistory.org

EXETER

American Independence Museum   The American Independence Museum traces the role of Exeter, New Hampshire, and the Gilman family in the American Revolution.

Address: One Governors Lane, Exeter, NH 03833
Phone: 306-772-2622
Web Site: www.independencemuseum.org

GLEN

Heritage New Hampshire   Heritage New Hampshire allows people to go through 300 years of New Hampshire history.

Address: P.O. Box 1776, Glen, NH 03838
Phone: 603-383-4186
Web Site: www.heritagenh.com

MANCHESTER

General John Stark House   This house was lived in by General John Stark.

Address: 2000 Elm Street, Manchester, NH 03102
Phone: 603-622-5719

PORTSMOUTH

Portsmouth Black Heritage Trail   The Portsmouth Black Heritage Trail is a self-guided tour that traces Portsmouth's African-American history.

Address: P.O. Box 7158, Portsmouth, NH 03802
Phone: 603-427-2020
Web Site: www.seacoastnh.com/blackhistory/trail.html

Portsmouth Harbour Trail   This self-guided walking tour goes through Portsmouth's historic downtown.

Address: 500 Market Street, Portsmouth, NH 03801
Phone: 603-436-3988
Web Site: www.visitnh.gov/todo/html?action=
   showcategory@cat=14

Strawbery Banke Museum Strawbery Banke Museum is a collection of historic houses that are open to the public.

Address: P.O. Box 300, Portsmouth, NH 03802
Phone: 603-433-1100
Web Site: www.strawberybanke.org

WARNER

Mt. Kearsarge Indian Museum The Mt. Kearsarge Indian Museum offers guided tours that explore Native American history.

Address: Kearsarge Mountain Road, Warner, NH 03278
Phone: 603-456-2600
Web Site: www.indianmuseum.org

WOLFEBORO

Governor John Wentworth Historic Site Governor John Wentworth, the state's last colonial governor, made this his summer house.

Address: P.O. Box 1578, Wolfeboro, NH 03894
Phone: 603-436-1552

Further Reading

BOOKS

Blohm, Craig E. *The Thirteen Colonies: New Hampshire.* San Diego, Calif.: Lucent, 2002.

Daniell, Jere R. *Colonial New Hampshire.* Millwood, N.Y.: KTO Press, 1981.

Fradin, Dennis B. *The New Hampshire Colony.* Chicago: Children's Press, 1988.

Giffen, Daniel H. *The New Hampshire Colony.* New York: Crowell-Collier, 1970.

Wyborny, Sheila. *New Hampshire.* San Diego, Calif.: Kidhaven Press, 2003.

WEB SITES

New Hampshire Historical Society. "Museum of New Hampshire History." Available online. URL: www.nhhistory.org. Downloaded on January 24, 2004.

New Hampshire State Library. "New Hampshire Almanac: A Brief History of New Hampshire." Available online. URL: www.state.nh.us/nhinfo/history.html. Downloaded on December 27, 2003.

"Seacoast History." Available online. URL: www.seacoastnh.com/history/index.html. Downloaded on January 24, 2004.

University of New Hampshire. "The Capture of Fort William &
Mary, New Castle, New Hampshire, December 14–15, 1774."
Available online. URL: www.izaak.unh.edu/exhibits/1774/.
Downloaded on December 27, 2003.

Index

Page numbers in *italic* indicate photographs. Page numbers in **boldface** indicate box features. Page numbers followed by m indicate maps. Page numbers followed by c indicate time line entries. Page numbers followed by t indicate tables or graphs.

House of Representatives, U.S. 102
houses, summer **59**
Howe, William 86–88
hunting 7–9
Hutchinson, Anne 20, 20

I

immune systems of Native Americans **12**
imports, Townshend Duties and 76
independence, New Hampshire declaration of 88–90
individualism 104
inflation 97
internal tax 76
Intolerable Acts. *See* Coercive Acts
Ireland 39, **64**
Iroquois, Lake of the 17
Iroquois League 13
Isles of Shoals 1, 2, **18,** 19, 105c

J

Jacques, Richard **55**
James II (duke of York and Albany, king of England) **44,** 45–49, 46, **46**
Jefferson, Thomas **89,** 89
Jocelyn, Henry 19
Jones, John Paul 94, 94, 95, **95,** 109c

K

Kearsarge Mountain Indian Museum (Warner, New Hampshire) 113
Kennebec River 19, **55**
Kennebec River colony **14**
kickbacks, Benning Wentworth and 59
kidnapping, of Native Americans **27**
King George's War 66–68
King Philip's War 29–34, 31–33, **34**
King's Woods 55
King William's War 51–53
Kingwood (Wolfeboro), New Hampshire 108c

L

Labrador **18**
Laconia Company 17, 19
land claims 14–17, 65. *See also* boundary disputes
land grants
    Bow, New Hampshire 65
    Council of New England 15
    Gorges's and Mason's 15–17, 16m
    James II's **46**
    Londonderry 62–64
    Massachusetts 62
    Rumford 64–65
    Benning Wentworth and 58
    John Wentworth II and 61
Langdon, John 101
    Constitutional Convention 102
    Continental army 90
    Second Continental Congress 88
    William and Mary, Fort 81
laws 42, **43,** 99
League of the Iroquois 13
Lebanon, Connecticut **60**
Leonardson, Samuel **53**
Letters of Marque and Reprisal 96
Lexington and Concord, Battles of 83
lieutenant governor
    Edward Cranfield 43–44, **44**
    John Wentworth 57–58, 107c
Little Harbor. *See* Pannaway
Livingston, Robert 89
Londonderry, New Hampshire 62–65, **70, 85,** 107c
Long Island 20
Louisbourg, Battle of **67,** 67, **67,** 107c
Loyalists 61, 77, **77, 79**
lumber industry 55–57
    Caribbean trade 50
    first settlers 17, 19
    trade with England 49
    Benning Wentworth and 58–59
Luther, Martin xiv

M

magistrates **43**
Maine, Province of 16m
    fishing camps 1
    Ferdinando Gorges and **14**
    Mason's and Gorges's land grants 15–16, 105c
    and Massachusetts colonial charter 49
    splitting of 19
Maine, State of **64**
maize (corn) **6**
Manchester, New Hampshire 3
maple syrup 5
maple trees 5
mapping, of New England 1
Marianna Grant 16–17, 20–21
marriage, in Western Abenaki society 10–11
Mary II (queen of England) 52
Mason, John (1586–1635) **15**
    Council of New England 15
    Danish cattle 19
    heirs' claims 40, **40,** 43–44
    land grants 16m, 105c–106c
    Marianna Grant 21
    Pannaway settlement 106c
    planning and development of New Hampshire colony 17, 19
    Province of Maine 19
Mason, John (1600–1672) 25
Massachusetts
    border disputes 21–22, 29, 57–58
    circulation petition to rejoin 49
    claims on New Hampshire towns (1641) 21–22, **37**
    conflicts over rights to settle land 62
    Joseph Dudley 107c
    early growth of 19–20
    Londonderry land grant 63
    model for New Hampshire Constitution 101
    Nashua Indians 2
    New England Confederation 28, 29

paper money 97, 97
Paris, Treaty of (1763) 71, 107c
Paris, Treaty of (1783) 96
Parliament
    Charles I and 35
    Charles II and **39**
    Coercive (Intolerable) Acts 78, 79
    First Continental Congress 80, **80**
    Battles of Lexington and Concord 84
    Stamp Act 73
    Sugar Act 72
    Townshend Duties 76
Patriots
    capture of Fort William and Mary 80–82
    Green Mountain Boys **92**
    Battles of Lexington and Concord 83
Pawtucket Falls, New Hampshire 65
Pennacook, New Hampshire 65
Pennacook Indians 3, **34,** 51, 106c
Pepperell, William **67**
Pequot village 25
Pequot War 23–26, 28
Philadelphia 80, 89, 102
Philip, King. *See* King Philip's War; Metacom
Piscataqua Indians 2
Piscataqua River
    fish stages 19
    Newichawannock 17
    Pannaway settlement 106c
    Martin Pring's expedition 2, 105c
    Province of Maine 19
Plymouth Colony
    border disputes 29, 30
    early growth of 20
    Fernando Gorges and **14**
    King Philip's War 30
    New England Confederation 28
    Martin Pring's expedition 2
Plymouth Company 17

Pocumtuc Indians 31
popcorn **6**
population
    effect of King William's War on 53
    Native Americans (1670) 106c
    New England colonists (1670) 29
    New Hampshire and Massachusetts (1630–1640) 19–20
    New Hampshire and Massachusetts (1680) 41
    New Hampshire growth (1630–1790) 63t
    New Hampshire growth (1710–1740) 62
portages 6
Portland, Maine 63
Portsmouth, New Hampshire 22m
    center of one area of colony 62
    Committee of Correspondence 108c
    Continental navy 93
    first settlement of 17
    lumber 49, 55, 57
    privateers 96
    ratification of U.S. Constitution 104
    Paul Revere's ride to 80–81
    Stamp Act protests 75
Portsmouth Black Heritage Trail 112
Portsmouth Harbour Trail 112
Portsmouth Navy Yard 93
potato 64, **64**
"Praying Indians" (Christian Indians)
    French and Indian War 71
    King Philip's War 29, 32
    John Sassamon 30
    John Stark and **85**
Presbyterians 62–64
Prescott, William 86
Pring, Martin 2, 105c
prisoners 65
prisoners of war 52
privateers 96

Privy Council 44, **92**
Protestant Reformation xiv–xv
Protestants xiv–xvi, 43, 54
protests, Stamp Act 73, 74
Providence Colony 20, 27
Province of Maine. *See* Maine, province of
Province of New Hampshire 41, 43, 106c
provincial assembly
    dissolution by Wentworth 80, 108c
    establishment of government 42
    and New Hampshire Constitution 88–89
    and Second Continental Congress 88
provincial congress 80
provisional government 109c
Puritans
    Charles I and 35
    Charles II and **39**
    Oliver Cromwell and 37
    in England 35–37
    and Native Americans 23, **27, 28**
    in New Hampshire 21
    religious intolerance of 20
    satirical drawing of 36
    and voting rights **37**

Q

Quartering Act of 1765 79, **79**
Quebec, Canada 71
Queen Anne's War 53–55, 65, 66
Queen's American Rangers **70**

R

racial intolerance 29
Raleigh (ship) 93
Ranger (ship) 93, 94
Rasle, Father Sébastien **55**
ratification, of U. S. Constitution 102–104, 104
Ratifying Convention, New Hampshire **103**
redcoats 86. *See also* British army
regionalism 101